MAX LUCADO

LIFE LESSONS *from*

HEBREWS

The Incomparable Christ

PREPARED BY THE LIVINGSTONE CORPORATION

THOMAS NELSON
Since 1798

Life Lessons from Hebrews

Copyright © 2018 by Max Lucado

Published in Nashville, Tennessee, by Thomas Nelson. Thomas Nelson is a registered trademark of HarperCollins Christian Publishing, Inc.

Produced with the assistance of the Livingstone Corporation (www.livingstonecorp.com). Project staff include Jake Barton, Joel Bartlett, Andy Culbertson, and Mary Horner Collins.

Editor: Neil Wilson

All Scripture quotations, unless otherwise indicated, are taken from The Holy Bible, New International Version®, NIV®. Copyright © 1973, 1978, 1984, 2011 by Biblica, Inc.™ Used by permission. All rights reserved worldwide. www.Zondervan.com. The "NIV" and "New International Version" are trademarks registered in the United States Patent and Trademark Office by Biblica, Inc.®

Scripture quotations marked NKJV are taken from the New King James Version®. Copyright © 1982 by Thomas Nelson. Used by permission. All rights reserved.

Material for the "Inspiration" sections taken from the following books:

3:16: The Numbers of Hope. © 2007 by Max Lucado. Thomas Nelson, a registered trademark of HarperCollins Christian Publishing, Inc., Nashville, Tennessee.

Cast of Characters. © 2008 by Max Lucado. Thomas Nelson, a registered trademark of HarperCollins Christian Publishing, Inc., Nashville, Tennessee.

Glory Days. Copyright © 2015 by Max Lucado. Thomas Nelson, a registered trademark of HarperCollins Christian Publishing, Inc., Nashville, Tennessee.

God Came Near. Copyright © 2004 by Max Lucado. Thomas Nelson, a registered trademark of HarperCollins Christian Publishing, Inc., Nashville, Tennessee.

Grace. Copyright © 2012 by Max Lucado. Thomas Nelson, a registered trademark of HarperCollins Christian Publishing, Inc., Nashville, Tennessee.

It's Not About Me. Copyright © 2004 by Max Lucado. Thomas Nelson, a registered trademark of HarperCollins Christian Publishing, Inc., Nashville, Tennessee.

Next Door Savior. Copyright © 2003 by Max Lucado. Thomas Nelson, a registered trademark of HarperCollins Christian Publishing, Inc., Nashville, Tennessee.

Shaped by God (previously published as *On the Anvil*). Copyright © 2001 by Max Lucado. Tyndale House Publishers, Inc, Carol Stream, Illinois.

Six Hours One Friday. Copyright © 2004 by Max Lucado. Thomas Nelson, a registered trademark of HarperCollins Christian Publishing, Inc., Nashville, Tennessee.

Unshakable Hope. Copyright © 2018 by Max Lucado. Thomas Nelson, a registered trademark of HarperCollins Christian Publishing, Inc., Nashville, Tennessee.

Walking with Christ in the Details of Life. Copyright © 1992 by Patrick Morley. Thomas Nelson, a registered trademark of HarperCollins Christian Publishing, Inc., Nashville, Tennessee.

Thomas Nelson titles may be purchased in bulk for educational, business, fundraising, or sales promotional use. For information, please e-mail SpecialMarkets@ThomasNelson.com.

ISBN 978-0-310-08658-1

First Printing October 2018 / Printed in the United States of America

CONTENTS

HOW TO STUDY THE BIBLE

The Bible is a peculiar book. Words crafted in another language. Deeds done in a distant era. Events recorded in a far-off land. Counsel offered to a foreign people. It is a peculiar book.

It's surprising that anyone reads it. It's too old. Some of its writings date back 5,000 years. It's too bizarre. The book speaks of incredible floods, fires, earthquakes, and people with supernatural abilities. It's too radical. The Bible calls for undying devotion to a carpenter who called himself God's Son.

Logic says this book shouldn't survive. Too old, too bizarre, too radical.

The Bible has been banned, burned, scoffed, and ridiculed. Scholars have mocked it as foolish. Kings have branded it as illegal. A thousand times over the grave has been dug and the dirge has begun, but somehow the Bible never stays in the grave. Not only has it survived, but it has also thrived. It is the single most popular book in all of history. It has been the bestselling book in the world for years!

There is no way on earth to explain it. Which perhaps is the only explanation. For the Bible's durability is not found on *earth* but in *heaven*. The millions who have tested its claims and claimed its promises know there is but one answer: the Bible is God's book and God's voice.

As you read it, you would be wise to give some thought to two questions: *What is the purpose of the Bible?* and *How do I study the Bible?* Time spent reflecting on these two issues will greatly enhance your Bible study.

What is the purpose of the Bible?

Let the Bible itself answer that question: *"From infancy you have known the Holy Scriptures, which are able to make you wise for salvation through faith in Christ Jesus"* (2 Timothy 3:15).

The purpose of the Bible? Salvation. God's highest passion is to get his children home. His book, the Bible, describes his plan of salvation. The purpose of the Bible is to proclaim God's plan and passion to save his children.

This is the reason why this book has endured through the centuries. It dares to tackle the toughest questions about life: *Where do I go after I die? Is there a God? What do I do with my fears?* The Bible is the treasure map that leads to God's highest treasure—eternal life.

But how do you study the Bible? Countless copies of Scripture sit unread on bookshelves and nightstands simply because people don't know how to read it. What can you do to make the Bible real in your life?

The clearest answer is found in the words of Jesus: *"Ask and it will be given to you; seek and you will find; knock and the door will be opened to you"* (Matthew 7:7).

The first step in understanding the Bible is asking God to help you. You should read it prayerfully. If anyone understands God's Word, it is because of God and not the reader.

"The Advocate, the Holy Spirit, whom the Father will send in my name, will teach you all things and will remind you of everything I have said to you" (John 14:26).

Before reading the Bible, pray and invite God to speak to you. Don't go to Scripture looking for your idea, but go searching for his.

Not only should you read the Bible prayerfully, but you should also read it carefully. *"Seek and you will find"* is the pledge. The Bible is not a newspaper to be skimmed but rather a mine to be quarried. *"If you look for it as for silver and search for it as for hidden treasure, then you will understand the fear of the LORD and find the knowledge of God"* (Proverbs 2:4–5).

Any worthy find requires effort. The Bible is no exception. To understand the Bible, you don't have to be brilliant, but you must be willing to roll up your sleeves and search.

"Do your best to present yourself to God as one approved, a worker who does not need to be ashamed and who correctly handles the word of truth" (2 Timothy 2:15).

Here's a practical point. Study the Bible a bit at a time. Hunger is not satisfied by eating twenty-one meals in one sitting once a week. The body needs a steady diet to remain strong. So does the soul. When God sent food to his people in the wilderness, he didn't provide loaves already made. Instead, he sent them manna in the shape of *"thin flakes like frost on the ground"* (Exodus 16:14).

God gave manna in limited portions.

God sends spiritual food the same way. He opens the heavens with just enough nutrients for today's hunger. He provides *"a rule for this, a rule for that; a little here, a little there"* (Isaiah 28:10).

Don't be discouraged if your reading reaps a small harvest. Some days a lesser portion is all that is needed. What is important is to search every day for that day's message. A steady diet of God's Word over a lifetime builds a healthy soul and mind.

It's much like the little girl who returned from her first day at school feeling a bit dejected. Her mom asked, "Did you learn anything?"

"Apparently not enough," the girl responded. "I have to go back tomorrow, and the next day, and the next . . . "

Such is the case with learning. And such is the case with Bible study. Understanding comes little by little over a lifetime.

There is a third step in understanding the Bible. After the asking and seeking comes the knocking. After you ask and search, *"knock and the door will be opened to you"* (Matthew 7:7).

To knock is to stand at God's door. To make yourself available. To climb the steps, cross the porch, stand at the doorway, and volunteer. Knocking goes beyond the realm of thinking and into the realm of acting.

To knock is to ask, *What can I do? How can I obey? Where can I go?*

It's one thing to know what to do. It's another to do it. But for those who do it—those who choose to obey—a special reward awaits them.

"Whoever looks intently into the perfect law that gives freedom, and continues in it—not forgetting what they have heard, but doing it—they will be blessed in what they do" (James 1:25).

What a promise. Blessings come to those who do what they read in God's Word! It's the same with medicine. If you only read the label but ignore the pills, it won't help. It's the same with food. If you only read the recipe but never cook, you won't be fed. And it's the same with the Bible. If you only read the words but never obey, you'll never know the joy God has promised.

Ask. Search. Knock. Simple, isn't it? So why don't you give it a try? If you do, you'll see why the Bible is the most remarkable book in history.

INTRODUCTION TO
The Book of Hebrews

The best just got better—it's a favorite slogan with advertisers.

It's not that our previous product was poor. It's just that the current one is superior.

The book of Hebrews might well use the same slogan. The best just got better.

There was nothing inferior about the Jewish religion. It was given by God and designed by God. Every principle, rule, and ritual had a wealth of meaning. The Old Testament served as a faithful guide for thousands of people over thousands of years. It was the best offered to man.

But when Christ came, the best got better.

Hebrews was written for Jewish believers who were torn between their new faith and their old ways. The temptation was to slip back into familiar routines and rituals, settling for second best.

The author skillfully makes a case against such a digression. He argues that Jesus is better than every form of the old faith—better than the angels, better than the believers' leaders, and better than their priests. When it comes to comparing the two, there is simply no comparison.

Christianity has a better covenant, a better sanctuary, and a better sacrifice for sins.

It's not that the old law was bad; it's just that the new law—salvation by faith in Christ—is better. Once you've known the best, why settle for second rate?

It's doubtful that you will ever be tempted to exchange your faith for an ancient system of priests and sacrifices. But you will be tempted to exchange it for something inferior. If you are reading Hebrews, be reminded: Once you've known the best, why settle for anything less? (Hmmm, there's another catchy slogan.)

AUTHOR AND DATE

It is not known who wrote the book of Hebrews. In the earliest surviving manuscripts of the New Testament (c. AD 200) it is placed with Paul's letters, but even church fathers such as Irenaeus and Hippolytus doubted it was actually penned by the apostle. Tertullian, writing at the beginning of the third century, claimed it was written by Barnabas, while Origen believed it was written by a close follower of Paul. During the Reformation period, Martin Luther proposed the writer was Apollos, a Jewish Christian who was instructed by Priscilla and Aquila in the city Ephesus (see Acts 18:24–28). This identification fits well with what can be gleaned from the letter about the author's identity—male, Jewish, well schooled in the Old Testament, and an eloquent writer of classical Greek—and today this is the favored view of authorship. Regarding the date of composition, given the fact the author focuses on a new approach to God that replaces the old sacrificial system— but makes no mention of the destruction of the Temple in Jerusalem in AD 70—it can be assumed the letter was penned prior to that date.

SITUATION

While the intended recipients of Hebrews are also unknown, it can be assumed they were a community firmly grounded in the Old Testament who identified themselves with the history and ideology of the Jewish people. It has been widely suggested these recipients were Jewish

Christians based in Rome, due in part to the author's comment that he was with "those from Italy" who sent their greetings (Hebrews 13:24). It is clear the author feels this particular group of Jewish Christians is in danger of drifting away from their faith, due not only to the persecutions they are facing but also their own uncertainty as to whether they made the correct decision in choosing to follow Jesus. To address these concerns, the author shows how everything that made up the Old Testament covenant—the prophets, laws, priesthood, temple and everything else—has been succeeded by something *better* and *greater* in Christ.

KEY THEMES

- Jesus Christ brought about a whole new way of connecting with and following God.
- Jesus is our compassionate high priest.
- Faith is the connector between this life and the next.

KEY VERSE

Jesus, the author and finisher of our faith . . . endured the cross, despising the shame, and has sat down at the right hand of the throne of God (Hebrews 12:2 NKJV).

CONTENTS

JESUS UNDERSTANDS US

*For in that He Himself has suffered, being tempted,
He is able to aid those who are tempted.*
HEBREWS 2:18 NKJV

REFLECTION

All of encounter pain and disappointments at some point in our lives. Some of these last for a brief time, while others stay with us for lifetime. Think for a moment about how you cope with difficulties. Where do you usually turn for comfort when you are hurting?

SITUATION

The writer of Hebrews wanted to highlight the uniqueness of Christ. From the first sentence of his letter to the last, he presents Jesus as the final word from God and reveals how he is superior everything else. The author begins by showing how Jesus is higher than the angels. At the time in Jewish culture there was a great fascination with angels, but the author wants to make it clear these heavenly beings pale in comparison to God's Son. The writer's point is not to disparage angels but demonstrate the surpassing greatness of Christ and his effective ministry on behalf of those he came to save.

OBSERVATION

Read Hebrews 2:10–18 from the New International Version or the New King James Version.

NEW INTERNATIONAL VERSION

[10] In bringing many sons and daughters to glory, it was fitting that God, for whom and through whom everything exists, should make the pioneer of their salvation perfect through what he suffered. [11] Both the one who makes people holy and those who are made holy are of the same family. So Jesus is not ashamed to call them brothers and sisters. [12] He says,

> "I will declare your name to my brothers and sisters;
>   in the assembly I will sing your praises."

[13] And again,

> "I will put my trust in him."

And again he says,

> "Here am I, and the children God has given me."

[14] Since the children have flesh and blood, he too shared in their humanity so that by his death he might break the power of him who holds the power of death—that is, the devil— [15] and free those who all their lives were held in slavery by their fear of death. [16] For surely it is not angels he helps, but Abraham's descendants. [17] For this reason he had to be made

like them, fully human in every way, in order that he might become a merciful and faithful high priest in service to God, and that he might make atonement for the sins of the people. [18] Because he himself suffered when he was tempted, he is able to help those who are being tempted.

NEW KING JAMES VERSION

[10] For it was fitting for Him, for whom are all things and by whom are all things, in bringing many sons to glory, to make the captain of their salvation perfect through sufferings. [11] For both He who sanctifies and those who are being sanctified are all of one, for which reason He is not ashamed to call them brethren, [12] saying:

> "I will declare Your name to My brethren;
> In the midst of the assembly I will sing praise to You."

[13] And again:

> "I will put My trust in Him."

And again:

> "Here am I and the children whom God has given Me."

[14] Inasmuch then as the children have partaken of flesh and blood, He Himself likewise shared in the same, that through death He might destroy him who had the power of death, that is, the devil, [15] and release those who through fear of death were all their lifetime subject to bondage. [16] For indeed He does not give aid to angels, but He does give aid to the seed of Abraham. [17] Therefore, in all things He had to be made like His brethren, that He might be a merciful and faithful High Priest in things pertaining to God, to make propitiation for the sins of the people. [18] For in that He Himself has suffered, being tempted, He is able to aid those who are tempted.

EXPLORATION

1. According to this passage, why did God allow his Son to suffer?

2. How does Jesus see those who choose to put their faith in him?

3. What effect did Jesus' victory over death have on Satan?

4. What can free people from their fear of death?

5. Why did Jesus have to come to this world in human form?

_____

_____

_____

_____

6. In what ways is Jesus able to help you because of what he endured on this earth?

_____

_____

_____

_____

INSPIRATION

Abandon. Such a haunting word.

On the edge of the small town sits a decrepit house. Weeds higher than the porch. Boarded windows and a screen door bouncing in the wind. To the front gate is nailed a sign: *Abandoned.* No one wants the place. Even the poor and desperate pass it by.

A social worker appears at the door of an orphanage. In her big hand is the small dirty one of a six-year-old girl. As the adults speak, the wide eyes of the child explore the office of the director. She hears the worker whisper, "Abandoned. She was abandoned."

An elderly woman in a convalescent home rocks alone in her room on Christmas. No cards, no calls, no carols.

A young wife discovers romantic e-mails sent by her husband to another woman.

After thirty years on the factory line, a worker finds a termination notice taped to his locker.

Abandoned by family. Abandoned by a spouse. Abandoned by big business.

But nothing compares to being abandoned by God.

"From noon until three in the afternoon darkness came over all the land. About three in the afternoon Jesus cried out in a loud voice, *"Eli, Eli, lema sabachthani?"*(which means "My God, my God, why have you forsaken me?") (Matthew 27:45–46).

By the time Christ screams these words, he has hung on the cross for six hours. Around nine o'clock in the morning, he stumbled to the cleft of Skull Hill. A soldier pressed a knee on his forearm and drove a spike through one hand, then the other, then both feet. As the Romans lifted the cross, they unwittingly placed Christ in the very position in which he came to die—between man and God.

A priest on his own altar. (From *Next Door Savior* by Max Lucado.)

REACTION

7. What experiences in your life comes to mind when you hear the word *abandoned*?

_____

_____

_____

_____

8. How was the suffering Jesus faced on the cross greater than any trials you will face?

_____

_____

_____

9. How does it help when you feel abandoned to know that Jesus can relate to you?

_____

_____

_____

_____

_____

10. How should you as a believer respond to the pain that comes your way?

_____

_____

_____

_____

_____

11. How has knowing Jesus increased your sensitivity to and compassion for others?

_____

_____

_____

_____

_____

12. What can you do to show God's love to someone who is hurting?

_____

_____

_____

_____

LIFE LESSONS

One of the times we tend to feel alone is when we are facing temptation. It's common for us to think our struggle is unique and that we are all alone. But this passage in Hebrews reminds us that Jesus knows what we face. He "gets" it. He has faced the same temptations. He knows our situation—and he understands. He wants to help. Will you let him?

DEVOTION

Jesus, we stand in awe of what you have done for us. You left your throne to live among us; you faced temptation, ridicule, and shame so you could understand us; and then you died on a cross to save us from our sins. You gave up everything so we could spend eternity with you. Help us to grasp the depth of your love—and to share that love with others.

JOURNALING

How has Jesus shown his love for you? How can you thank him today for his love?

_____

_____

_____

_____

_____

_____

_____

_____

_____

_____

_____

FOR FURTHER READING

To complete the book of Hebrews during this twelve-part study, read Hebrews 1:1–2:18. For more Bible passages about Jesus' ability to help hurting people, read Job 36:15; Psalms 46:1; 121:1–2; 147:1–5; Isaiah 41:10; 53:3–5; and Romans 8:26–27.

KEEP THE FAITH

*See to it, brothers and sisters, that none of you has
a sinful, unbelieving heart that turns away from the
living God. But encourage one another daily.*
<small>HEBREWS 3:12–13</small>

REFLECTION

Think about a time when a Christian friend encouraged you in your faith. What was your situation at the time? What specific actions or statements did the person use to help you? What have been the long-term results in your life of that person's ministry?

SITUATION

The author of Hebrews, having shown why Jesus is superior to the angels, now explores why Jesus is superior to the kings, priests, leaders, and prophets of the Old Testament. He begins with Moses—the giver of God's Law—who in the hierarchy of heroes in Israel's history had no equal. To the Jewish people, Moses exhibited every aspect of strong spiritual and moral leadership. He had led the people out of Egypt, provided guidance from God in the midst of their bickering and complaining, and had continued to lead them even after they rebelled against God and were forced to wander in the wilderness. It is an impressive résumé—and yet the writer of Hebrews says Moses was nothing compared to Jesus. Furthermore, just as Christ was faithful to God's purposes, so should we—his followers—keep the faith to the end.

OBSERVATION

Read Hebrews 3:1–14 from the New International
Version or the New King James Version.

NEW INTERNATIONAL VERSION

[1] Therefore, holy brothers and sisters, who share in the heavenly calling, fix your thoughts on Jesus, whom we acknowledge as our apostle and high priest. [2] He was faithful to the one who appointed him, just as Moses was faithful in all God's house. [3] Jesus has been found worthy of greater honor than Moses, just as the builder of a house has greater honor than the house itself. [4] For every house is built by someone, but God is the builder of everything. [5] "Moses was faithful as a servant in all God's house," bearing witness to what would be spoken by God in the future. [6] But Christ is faithful as the Son over God's house. And we are his house, if indeed we hold firmly to our confidence and the hope in which we glory.

[7] So, as the Holy Spirit says:

"Today, if you hear his voice,
[8] do not harden your hearts
as you did in the rebellion,
during the time of testing in the wilderness,
[9] where your ancestors tested and tried me,
though for forty years they saw what I did.
[10] That is why I was angry with that generation;
I said, 'Their hearts are always going astray,
and they have not known my ways.'
[11] So I declared on oath in my anger,
'They shall never enter my rest.'"

[12] See to it, brothers and sisters, that none of you has a sinful, unbelieving heart that turns away from the living God. [13] But encourage one

another daily, as long as it is called "Today," so that none of you may be hardened by sin's deceitfulness. [14] We have come to share in Christ, if indeed we hold our original conviction firmly to the very end.

NEW KING JAMES VERSION

[1] Therefore, holy brethren, partakers of the heavenly calling, consider the Apostle and High Priest of our confession, Christ Jesus, [2] who was faithful to Him who appointed Him, as Moses also was faithful in all His house. [3] For this One has been counted worthy of more glory than Moses, inasmuch as He who built the house has more honor than the house. [4] For every house is built by someone, but He who built all things is God. [5] And Moses indeed was faithful in all His house as a servant, for a testimony of those things which would be spoken afterward, [6] but Christ as a Son over His own house, whose house we are if we hold fast the confidence and the rejoicing of the hope firm to the end.

[7] Therefore, as the Holy Spirit says:

"Today, if you will hear His voice,
[8] Do not harden your hearts as in the rebellion,
In the day of trial in the wilderness,
[9] Where your fathers tested Me, tried Me,
And saw My works forty years.
[10] Therefore I was angry with that generation,
And said, 'They always go astray in their heart,
And they have not known My ways.'
[11] So I swore in My wrath,
'They shall not enter My rest.'"

[12] Beware, brethren, lest there be in any of you an evil heart of unbelief in departing from the living God; [13] but exhort one another daily, while it is called "Today," lest any of you be hardened through the deceitfulness of sin. [14] For we have become partakers of Christ if we hold the beginning of our confidence steadfast to the end.

EXPLORATION

1. What does it mean to "fix your thoughts on Jesus" (verse 1)?

_____

_____

_____

_____

2. Why is Jesus worthy of greater honor than Moses?

_____

_____

_____

3. How can you demonstrate that you belong in "God's house"?

_____

_____

_____

_____

4. What warning does the Holy Spirit give to you in this passage?

_____

_____

_____

_____

5. Why do some people turn away from God?

6. What practical advice does this passage offer on remaining faithful to God?

INSPIRATION

God invites us to enter Canaan. There is only one condition. We must turn our backs on the wilderness. Just as Canaan represents the *victorious* Christian life, the wilderness represents the *defeated* Christian life. In the desert the Hebrew people were liberated from Egyptian bondage, but you wouldn't have known it by listening to them. . . .

"The people contended with Moses" (Exodus 17:2 NKJV), and "the people complained against Moses" (verse 3 NKJV). They inhaled anxiety like oxygen. They bellyached to the point that Moses prayed, "What shall I do with this people? They are almost ready to stone me!" (verse 4 NKJV).

How did the Hebrews descend to this point? It wasn't for the lack of miracles. They saw God's power in high definition. They watched locusts gobble crops, boils devour skin, flies buzz through Pharaoh's court. God turned the chest-thumping Egyptians into shark bait right before the Hebrews' eyes.

But when God called them to cross over into Canaan, the twelve spies returned, and all but two said the mission was impossible. The giants were too big for them. "We seemed like grasshoppers," they said (Numbers 13:33). *We were tiny, tiny bugs. They will squash us.*

So God gave them time to think it over. He put the entire nation in time-out for nearly forty years. They walked in circles. They ate the same food every day. Life was an endless routine of the same rocks, lizards, and snakes. Victories were scarce. Progress was slow. They were saved but not strong. Redeemed but not released. Saved from Pharaoh but stuck in the desert. Redeemed but locked in a routine. Monotonous. Dull. Ho-hum, humdrum. Four decades of tedium.

Sounds miserable. It might sound familiar. . . .

Think about the Christian you want to be. What qualities do you want to have? More compassion? More conviction? More courage? What attitudes do you want to discontinue? Greed? Guilt? Endless negativity? A critical spirit?

Here is the good news. You can. With God's help you can close the gap between the person you are and the person you want to be, indeed, the person God made you to be. You can live "from glory to glory" (2 Corinthians 3:18 NKJV). The walls of Jericho are already condemned. The giants are already on the run. The deed to your new life in Canaan has already been signed.

It just falls to you to possess the land. (From *Glory Days* by Max Lucado.)

REACTION

7. Read Numbers 13:26–33. What report did the ten spies give?

_____

_____

_____

_____

_____

8. How did Caleb demonstrate that he had "kept the faith" regarding God's promises?

9. Who do you tend to be more like when faced with an overwhelming situation—the ten spies or Caleb? Why?

10. What can you do to ensure that your faith will endure?

11. How can you avoid hardening your heart against God?

12. What is the danger as a Christian in neglecting the fellowship of other believers?

_____

_____

_____

_____

_____

_____

_____

LIFE LESSONS

Both Moses and Christ serve as examples of faithfulness to God. The alternative attitude is described in the Bible as "hardening our heart." We know what this means even when we hear the expression for the first time—we've stiffened our wills, backs, and hearts against God and have refused to move forward. This was the case for the Israelites on the door of the Promised Land, and it is familiar territory for most of us as well. God is offering us his rest, but we refused to take the step of faith and possess the land. The author of Hebrews reminds us in this passage that we need to keep moving forward in Christ—and we need to get into the habit of encouraging others along the way. We can help each other toward faithfulness.

DEVOTION

Father, we ask you to deepen our faith in you. Give us the strength to withstand temptation, overcome doubt, and remain loyal to you. At the end of our lives, may we hear your words, "Well done, my good and faithful servant."

JOURNALING

What practical steps can you take this week to strengthen your faith in God?

_____

_____

_____

_____

_____

_____

_____

_____

_____

_____

_____

_____

_____

_____

_____

_____

_____

_____

FOR FURTHER READING

To complete the book of Hebrews during this twelve-part study, read Hebrews 3:1–19. For more Bible passages about remaining faithful, read Deuteronomy 11:13–18; 1 Samuel 12:24; 1 Kings 2:3–4; Proverbs 28:20; Matthew 25:19–23; 1 Corinthians 10:12–13; 3 John 1:3–5; and Revelation 2:10.

LESSON THREE

GOD'S REST

*There remains therefore a rest for the
people of God. For he who has entered
His rest has himself also ceased from
his works as God did from His.*

HEBREWS 4:9–10 NKJV

REFLECTION

Many people have misconceptions about what it means to find true peace. What does your life look like when peace reigns? When peace is lacking, what tends to be in its place? How would you summarize your personal understanding of peace?

_____

_____

_____

_____

_____

_____

_____

_____

_____

_____

_____

_____

_____

_____

_____

SITUATION

As the author of Hebrews continues to discuss Moses' leadership and the Israelites' experience in the wilderness, he makes it clear that God intended for his children to enter the Promised Land—a land of rest, peace, and plenty. However, due to their disobedience and stubbornness, that generation was not allowed to enter into that promised place of rest. The writer draws on this historical event, which all of his Jewish readers would have recognized, and uses it as an analogy for the deeper and broader "salvation rest" that God calls all his children to enter.

OBSERVATION

Read Hebrews 4:1–11 from the New International
Version or the New King James Version.

NEW INTERNATIONAL VERSION

[1] Therefore, since the promise of entering his rest still stands, let us be careful that none of you be found to have fallen short of it. [2] For we also have had the good news proclaimed to us, just as they did; but the message they heard was of no value to them, because they did not share the faith of those who obeyed. [3] Now we who have believed enter that rest, just as God has said,

> "So I declared on oath in my anger,
> 'They shall never enter my rest.'"

And yet his works have been finished since the creation of the world. [4] For somewhere he has spoken about the seventh day in these words: "On the seventh day God rested from all his works." [5] And again in the passage above he says, "They shall never enter my rest."

[6] Therefore since it still remains for some to enter that rest, and since those who formerly had the good news proclaimed to them did not go in because of their disobedience, [7] God again set a certain day, calling it "Today." This he did when a long time later he spoke through David, as in the passage already quoted:

> "Today, if you hear his voice,
> do not harden your hearts."

⁸ For if Joshua had given them rest, God would not have spoken later about another day. ⁹ There remains, then, a Sabbath-rest for the people of God; ¹⁰ for anyone who enters God's rest also rests from their works, just as God did from his. ¹¹ Let us, therefore, make every effort to enter that rest, so that no one will perish by following their example of disobedience.

New King James Version

¹ Therefore, since a promise remains of entering His rest, let us fear lest any of you seem to have come short of it. ² For indeed the gospel was preached to us as well as to them; but the word which they heard did not profit them, not being mixed with faith in those who heard it. ³ For we who have believed do enter that rest, as He has said:

> "So I swore in My wrath,
> 'They shall not enter My rest,'"

although the works were finished from the foundation of the world. ⁴ For He has spoken in a certain place of the seventh day in this way: "And God rested on the seventh day from all His works"; ⁵ and again in this place: "They shall not enter My rest."

⁶ Since therefore it remains that some must enter it, and those to whom it was first preached did not enter because of disobedience, ⁷ again He designates a certain day, saying in David, "Today," after such a long time, as it has been said:

> "Today, if you will hear His voice,
> Do not harden your hearts."

⁸ For if Joshua had given them rest, then He would not afterward have spoken of another day. ⁹ There remains therefore a rest for the people of God. ¹⁰ For he who has entered His rest has himself also ceased from his works as God did from His.

[11] Let us therefore be diligent to enter that rest, lest anyone fall according to the same example of disobedience.

EXPLORATION

1. How would you define "God's rest"?

_____

_____

_____

_____

_____

2. Why won't some people be helped by the gospel?

_____

_____

_____

_____

3. In what way did God set an example of rest for us?

_____

_____

_____

_____

4. How can people today enter into God's rest?

_____

_____

_____

_____

5. How can you know that God's rest is still to come in the future?

_____

_____

_____

_____

_____

_____

_____

6. What part of the Hebrew people's experience should you *avoid* following?

_____

_____

_____

_____

_____

_____

INSPIRATION

Sleep is determined to bring the day to a close and joy is determined to stretch the day out as long as possible. One last enchanted kingdom. One last giggle. One last game.

Maybe you are like that. Maybe, if you had your way, your day would never end. Every moment demands to be savored. You resist sleep as long as possible because you love being awake so much. If you are like that, congratulations. If not, welcome to the majority.

Most of us have learned another way of going to bed, haven't we? It's called crash and burn. Life is so full of games that the last thing we want is another one as we are trying to sleep. So, for most of us, it's good-bye world, hello pillow. Sleep, for many, is not a robber but a refuge; eight hours of relief for our wounded souls.

And if you are kept awake, it's not by counting your fingers, but by counting your debts, tasks, or even your tears.

You are tired. You are weary.

Weary of being slapped by the waves of broken dreams.

Weary of being stepped on and run over in the endless marathon to the top.

Weary of trusting in someone only to have that trust returned in an envelope with no return address.

Weary of staring into the future and seeing only futility. . . .

It is this weariness that makes the words of the carpenter so compelling. Listen to them. "Come to me, all you who are weary and burdened, and I will give you rest" (Matthew 11:28).

Come to me . . . the invitation is to come to him. Why him? He offers the invitation as a penniless rabbi in an oppressed nation. He has no connections with the authorities in Rome. He hasn't written a best-seller or earned a diploma.

Yet, he dares to look into the leathery faces of farmers and tired faces of housewives and offer rest. He looks into the disillusioned eyes of a bartender and makes this paradoxical promise: "Take my yoke upon you and learn from me, for I am gentle and humble in heart, and you will find rest for your souls" (verse 29).

The people came. They came out of the cul-de-sacs and office complexes of their existence and he gave them, not religion, not doctrine, not systems, but rest.

As a result, they called him Lord. As a result, they called him Savior.

Not so much because of what he said, but because of what he did. What he did on the cross during six hours, one Friday. (From *Six Hours One Friday* by Max Lucado.)

REACTION

7. Would you describe yourself as more of a "wish-this-day-would-never-end" person or a "crash-and-burn" type individual? Why did you answer as you did?

_____

_____

_____

_____

_____

8. What are some areas in your life right now where you need God's rest?

_____

_____

_____

_____

_____

9. What was so unique about Jesus' offer when the people came to him weary and burdened?

_____

_____

_____

_____

_____

10. What do you think keeps you from enjoying more of the rest that God offers?

_____

_____

_____

_____

_____

11. How is your life different since you first discovered peace with God?

_____

_____

_____

12. How would you explain God's rest to a person who does not know Christ?

_____

_____

_____

LIFE LESSONS

One of Jesus' specific promises to us has to do with peace: "Peace I leave with you, My peace I give to you; not as the world gives do I give to you. Let not your heart be troubled, neither let it be afraid" (John 14:27 NKJV). Although the world talks about wanting *peace*, we know that the peace we have in Christ is something entirely different. God's peace is the rest that comes when we know our lives and our future are in the hands of Someone who is far more capable than us. The world thinks peace is a state we create by our efforts, but Christ offers us peace and asks us to let nothing keep us from entering it. It's his peace that we get to enjoy.

DEVOTION

We thank you, Father, that we can experience your rest both now and for all of eternity. Teach us to appreciate and enjoy the peace you offer today. Protect us from unbelief and disobedience so that nothing will keep us from entering into your eternal rest.

JOURNALING

What practical steps can you take this week to more fully enjoy God's rest?

FOR FURTHER READING

To complete the book of Hebrews during this twelve-part study, read Hebrews 4:1–13. For more Bible passages about God's rest, read Exodus 31:15–17; Psalms 16:9–11; 62:1–5; 95:10–11; 116:7; Isaiah 11:10; Jeremiah 6:16; Matthew 11:28–30; and Revelation 14:13.

JESUS, OUR HIGH PRIEST

Therefore, since we have a great high priest who has ascended into heaven, Jesus the Son of God, let us hold firmly to the faith we profess.

HEBREWS 4:14

REFLECTION

Some people believe they can't approach God on their own, but that author of Hebrews shows that we can approach God's throne directly, even boldly, through Jesus Christ. Think about your religious upbringing. What part did priests, pastors, or elders play in your church? When did you realize that, through Christ, you could have a relationship directly with God?

SITUATION

So far in his letter, the author has made a compelling argument as to why Jesus is superior to angels and the greatest leaders in Israel's history—including heroes such as Moses and Joshua. The writer now turns his examination to the Old Testament priesthood and system of sacrifices. As his Jewish readers would have acknowledged, the priests played a critical role in the people's worship to God. Of supreme importance was the high priest, who once a year was allowed to enter into the Most Holy Place in the Temple to make the atoning sacrifice for the people's sin. Without the high priest, no one could approach God, and no sacrifice for sin could be offered. Yet, as the writer will show, Jesus is greater than all of these high priests in Israel's history.

OBSERVATION

Read Hebrews 4:14–5:10 from the New International
Version or the New King James Version.

New International Version

⁴:¹⁴ Therefore, since we have a great high priest who has ascended into heaven, Jesus the Son of God, let us hold firmly to the faith we profess. ¹⁵ For we do not have a high priest who is unable to empathize with our weaknesses, but we have one who has been tempted in every way, just as we are—yet he did not sin. ¹⁶ Let us then approach God's throne of grace with confidence, so that we may receive mercy and find grace to help us in our time of need.

⁵:¹ Every high priest is selected from among the people and is appointed to represent the people in matters related to God, to offer gifts and sacrifices for sins. ² He is able to deal gently with those who are ignorant and are going astray, since he himself is subject to weakness. ³ This is why he has to offer sacrifices for his own sins, as well as for the sins of the people. ⁴ And no one takes this honor on himself, but he receives it when called by God, just as Aaron was.

⁵ In the same way, Christ did not take on himself the glory of becoming a high priest. But God said to him,

> "You are my Son;
>> today I have become your Father."

⁶ And he says in another place,

> "You are a priest forever,
>> in the order of Melchizedek."

⁷ During the days of Jesus' life on earth, he offered up prayers and petitions with fervent cries and tears to the one who could save him from

death, and he was heard because of his reverent submission. [8] Son though he was, he learned obedience from what he suffered [9] and, once made perfect, he became the source of eternal salvation for all who obey him [10] and was designated by God to be high priest in the order of Melchizedek.

NEW KING JAMES VERSION

[4:14] Seeing then that we have a great High Priest who has passed through the heavens, Jesus the Son of God, let us hold fast our confession. [15] For we do not have a High Priest who cannot sympathize with our weaknesses, but was in all points tempted as we are, yet without sin. [16] Let us therefore come boldly to the throne of grace, that we may obtain mercy and find grace to help in time of need.

[5:1] For every high priest taken from among men is appointed for men in things pertaining to God, that he may offer both gifts and sacrifices for sins. [2] He can have compassion on those who are ignorant and going astray, since he himself is also subject to weakness. [3] Because of this he is required as for the people, so also for himself, to offer sacrifices for sins. [4] And no man takes this honor to himself, but he who is called by God, just as Aaron was.

[5] So also Christ did not glorify Himself to become High Priest, but it was He who said to Him:

> "You are My Son,
> Today I have begotten You."

[6] As He also says in another place:

> "You are a priest forever
> According to the order of Melchizedek";

[7] who, in the days of His flesh, when He had offered up prayers and supplications, with vehement cries and tears to Him who was able to save Him from death, and was heard because of His godly fear, [8] though He

was a Son, yet He learned obedience by the things which He suffered. [9] And having been perfected, He became the author of eternal salvation to all who obey Him, [10] called by God as High Priest "according to the order of Melchizedek."

EXPLORATION

1. Why is it important that Jesus, as your high priest, can empathize with your weaknesses?

2. With what attitude should you approach God's throne in prayer? Why?

3. How would you describe the role and responsibilities of a high priest?

4. What qualified Jesus to become the ultimate high priest?

_____

_____

_____

_____

_____

5. Read Genesis 14:18–20 and Leviticus 16:3–16. In what ways was Jesus similar to Melchizedek and to other high priests like Aaron? How was he different?

_____

_____

_____

_____

_____

6. Why is Jesus able to offer you eternal salvation?

_____

_____

_____

_____

_____

INSPIRATION

You and I have . . . _have stumbled_. In morality, honesty, integrity. We have done our best, only to trip and fall. Our finest efforts have left us flat on our backs. We are weakened not with torn ligaments but with broken hearts, weary spirits, and fading vision. The distance between where we are and where we want to be is impassable. What do we do? Where do we turn?

I suggest we turn to one of the sweetest promises: "For we do not have a high priest who is unable to empathize with our weaknesses, but we have one who has been tempted in every way, just as we are—yet he did not sin. Let us then approach God's throne of grace with confidence, so that we may receive mercy and find grace to help us in our time of need" (Hebrews 4:15–16).

We have a high priest who is able to understand. Since he understands, we find mercy and grace when we need it. We are not left to languish. When we fall, we are not forgotten. When we stumble, we aren't abandoned. Our God gets us.

Theology textbooks discuss this promise under the heading "Incarnation." The stunning idea is simply this: God, for a time, became one of us. "The Word became flesh and made his dwelling among us. We have seen his glory, the glory of the one and only Son, who came from the Father, full of grace and truth" (John 1:14).

God became flesh in the form of Jesus Christ. He was miraculously conceived, yet naturally delivered. He was born, yet born of a virgin.

Had Jesus simply descended to earth in the form of a mighty being, we would respect him but never would draw near to him. After all, how could God understand what it means to be human?

Had Jesus been biologically conceived with two earthly parents, we would draw near to him, but would we want to worship him? After all, he would be no different than you and me.

But if Jesus was both—God and man at the same time—then we have the best of both worlds. Neither his humanity nor deity compromised. He was fully human. He was fully divine. Because of the first, we draw near. Because of the latter, we worship. . . .

Not one drop of divinity was lost in the change to humanity. Though Jesus appeared human, he was actually God. The fullness of God, every bit of him, took residence in the body of Christ. "For God was pleased to have all his fullness dwell in him" (Colossians 1:19). (From *Unshakable Hope* by Max Lucado.)

REACTION

7. How would you describe the concept of the Incarnation to someone?

_____

_____

_____

_____

8. Why is important that Jesus was both fully God and fully human?

_____

_____

_____

_____

9. What kind of relationship does Jesus want to have with you?

_____

_____

_____

_____

10. When have you felt reluctant to go to Jesus with a need or concern? Why?

_____

_____

_____

_____

11. How would your life be different if you released all of your problems to Jesus?

_____

_____

_____

_____

_____

12. What can you do to develop the habit of turning to God with your joys and concerns?

_____

_____

_____

_____

_____

LIFE LESSONS

The title _priest_ may convey a certain meaning for us when we consider their role as a mediators and representatives for us before God. But when such a title is applied to Jesus, it immediately carries more weight. First, it reminds us that Jesus _alone_ has the unique role of being both high priest and ultimate sacrifice. He did something we could never do: meet our own spiritual needs. Second, it reminds us of the cost involved in meeting those spiritual needs: Jesus gave his life for our sin. Third, it calls deep respect and obedience from us. The effectiveness of Jesus' work as our "high priest" is due to the fact he experienced real life among us and knows what we go through. In every way, Jesus is worthy of our trust with anything and everything.

DEVOTION

Father, you know our goals and dreams for the future, our deepest hurts and disappointments, and even our weaknesses and failures. You understand us completely. Teach us today to be open and honest with you—not for your benefit, but for ours.

JOURNALING

What have you held back from Jesus? How can you trust him with those parts of your life?

_____

_____

_____

_____

_____

_____

_____

_____

_____

_____

_____

_____

_____

FOR FURTHER READING

To complete the book of Hebrews during this twelve-part study, read Hebrews 4:14–5:14. For more Bible passages about Jesus' relationship with believers, read John 15:5; Romans 5:11; 1 Timothy 1:15; Hebrews 2:9–11; 6:19–20; 7:22–26; 8:1–2; and 1 Peter 2:4–10.

PERSEVERANCE

We desire that each one of you show the same diligence
to the full assurance of hope until the end, that
you do not become sluggish, but imitate those who
through faith and patience inherit the promises.

HEBREWS 6:11–12 NKJV

REFLECTION

The process of creating a vision, establishing a plan, setting goals, and pursuing them to completion can provide deep satisfaction for us. But one of the integral aspects of this process is our willingness to persevere to the end. Think of a time when you worked hard to reach a personal goal. What helped you persevere? How does that apply to your spiritual growth?

SITUATION

The author of Hebrews has demonstrated how Jesus is our "great high priest" (4:4) and how we can know he is able to emphasize with our weaknesses as human beings living in a fallen world. The writer now goes on a slight digression to challenge his readers to move toward greater maturity in Christ. He asks them to closely examine their actions and behaviors so they do not "become lazy" but persevere in the faith and thus "inherit what has been promised" (6:12). The writer's words apply to us today—we too must be diligent in continually moving toward spiritual maturity in Christ. We must actively receive all Jesus has done for us, make living for him our ultimate goal in life, and persevere in that high calling to the very end.

OBSERVATION

Read Hebrews 6:7–20 from the New International
Version or the New King James Version.

NEW INTERNATIONAL VERSION

[7] Land that drinks in the rain often falling on it and that produces a crop useful to those for whom it is farmed receives the blessing of God. [8] But land that produces thorns and thistles is worthless and is in danger of being cursed. In the end it will be burned.

[9] Even though we speak like this, dear friends, we are convinced of better things in your case—the things that have to do with salvation. [10] God is not unjust; he will not forget your work and the love you have shown him as you have helped his people and continue to help them. [11] We want each of you to show this same diligence to the very end, so that what you hope for may be fully realized. [12] We do not want you to become lazy, but to imitate those who through faith and patience inherit what has been promised.

[13] When God made his promise to Abraham, since there was no one greater for him to swear by, he swore by himself, [14] saying, "I will surely bless you and give you many descendants." [15] And so after waiting patiently, Abraham received what was promised.

[16] People swear by someone greater than themselves, and the oath confirms what is said and puts an end to all argument. [17] Because God wanted to make the unchanging nature of his purpose very clear to the heirs of what was promised, he confirmed it with an oath. [18] God did this so that, by two unchangeable things in which it is impossible for God

to lie, we who have fled to take hold of the hope set before us may be greatly encouraged. [19] We have this hope as an anchor for the soul, firm and secure. It enters the inner sanctuary behind the curtain, [20] where our forerunner, Jesus, has entered on our behalf. He has become a high priest forever, in the order of Melchizedek.

New King James Version

[7] For the earth which drinks in the rain that often comes upon it, and bears herbs useful for those by whom it is cultivated, receives blessing from God; [8] but if it bears thorns and briers, it is rejected and near to being cursed, whose end is to be burned.

[9] But, beloved, we are confident of better things concerning you, yes, things that accompany salvation, though we speak in this manner. [10] For God is not unjust to forget your work and labor of love which you have shown toward His name, in that you have ministered to the saints, and do minister. [11] And we desire that each one of you show the same diligence to the full assurance of hope until the end, [12] that you do not become sluggish, but imitate those who through faith and patience inherit the promises.

[13] For when God made a promise to Abraham, because He could swear by no one greater, He swore by Himself, [14] saying, "Surely blessing I will bless you, and multiplying I will multiply you." [15] And so, after he had patiently endured, he obtained the promise. [16] For men indeed swear by the greater, and an oath for confirmation is for them an end of all dispute. [17] Thus God, determining to show more abundantly to the heirs of promise the immutability of His counsel, confirmed it by an oath, [18] that by two immutable things, in which it is impossible for God to lie, we might have strong consolation, who have fled for refuge to lay hold of the hope set before us.

[19] This hope we have as an anchor of the soul, both sure and steadfast, and which enters the Presence behind the veil, [20] where the forerunner has entered for us, even Jesus, having become High Priest forever according to the order of Melchizedek.

EXPLORATION

1. How does the author of Hebrews compare a plot of land to a believer's life?

2. Whom does God bless? Whom does he curse? What results from God's blessings and curses?

3. How does God demonstrate his fairness to his people?

4. What promise has God given to his people? How can you know that promise is secure?

_____

_____

_____

5. Why is it encouraging to know that God's purposes never change?

_____

_____

_____

6. The author notes, "It is impossible for God to lie" (verse 18). What kind of security does that give you when it comes to the promises you find in the Bible?

_____

_____

_____

INSPIRATION

In the barren prairie, the hiker huddles down. The cold northerly sweeps over him, stinging his face and numbing his fingers. The whistle of the wind is deafening. The hiker hugs his knees to his chest, yearning for warmth.

He doesn't move. The sky is orange with dirt. His teeth are grainy, his eyes sooty. He thinks of quitting. Going home. Home to the mountains.

"Ahh. The mountains." The spirit that moved him in the mountains seems so far away. For a moment, his mind wanders back to his homeland. Green country. Mountain trails. Fresh water. Hikers hiking on well-marked trails. No surprises, few fears, rich companionship.

One day, while on a brisk hike, he had stopped to look out from the mountains across the neighboring desert. He felt strangely pulled to the sweeping barrenness that lay before him. The next day he paused again. And the next, and the next. "Shouldn't someone try to take life to the desert?" Slowly the flicker in his heart became a flame.

Many agreed that someone should go, but no one volunteered. Uncharted land, fearful storms, loneliness.

But the hiker, spurred by the enthusiasm of others, determined to go. After careful preparation, he set out, alone. With the cheers of his friends behind him, he descended the grassy highlands and entered the desolate wilderness.

The first few days his steps were springy and his eye was keen. He yearned to do his part to bring life to the desert. Then came the heat. The scorpions. The monotony. The snakes. Slowly, the fire diminished. And now . . . the storm. The endless roar of the wind. The relentless, cursed cold.

"I don't know how much more I can take." Weary and beaten, the hiker considers going back. "At least I got this far." Knees tucked under him, head bowed, almost touching the ground. "Will it ever stop?"

Grimly he laughs at the irony of the situation. "Some hiker. Too tired to go on, yet too ashamed to go home." Deep, deep is the struggle. No longer can he hear the voices of friends. Long gone is the romance of his mission. No longer does he float on the fancifulness of a dream.

"Maybe someone else should do this. I'm too young, too inexperienced." The winds of discouragement and fear whip at his fire, exhausting what is left of the flame. But the coals remain, hidden and hot.

The hiker, now almost the storm's victim, looks one last time for the fire. (Is there any greater challenge than of stirring a spirit while in the clutches of defeat?)

Yearning and clawing, the temptation to quit is gradually overcome by the urge to go on. Blowing on the coals, the hiker once again hears the call to the desert. Though faint, the call is clear.

With all the strength he can summon, the hiker rises to his feet, bows his head, and takes his first step into the wind. (From *Shaped by God* by Max Lucado.)

REACTION

7. As a believer in Christ, how would you define your primary goal in this life?

_____

_____

_____

_____

_____

8. What obstacles stand in the way of your fulfilling this goal?

_____

_____

_____

_____

_____

9. How can you prepare yourself to face and overcome those obstacles?

_____

_____

_____

_____

_____

10. What does it mean to trust in God's promises?

11. What are the rewards of trusting God?

12. Which of God's promises will you remember this week to help you persevere?

LIFE LESSONS

Persevering in our walk with God can be tough. But we don't have to do it alone. This passage in Hebrews reminds us of God's commitment to work in us and through us . . . much as the seed uses the soil to produce a great harvest. God kept his promise to Abraham, and he will keep his promise to us. He specializes in using weak things to accomplish his plan and demonstrate his power. We are the weak things. God has made a promise backed up by his character. We may fail to trust God, but God will never fail to be trustworthy!

DEVOTION

Father, help us to maintain our promise of faithfulness to you, even in times when we are filled with doubt, fear, and insecurity. Give us great courage to endure the storms that come our way. Help us press on toward the goal that you have set for us.

JOURNALING

What fears and doubts do you have? How does this passage challenge you to deal with those feelings?

_____

_____

_____

_____

_____

_____

_____

_____

_____

_____

FOR FURTHER READING

To complete the book of Hebrews during this twelve-part study, read Hebrews 6:1–7:28. For more Bible passages about perseverance, read Acts 20:24; Romans 5:3–4; 1 Timothy 4:16; 2 Timothy 2:12; Hebrews 10:36; James 1:2–4, 12; 5:11; Peter 1:5–11; and Revelation 2:2–3.

GOD FORGIVES AND FORGETS

For I will forgive their wickedness and will remember their sins no more.
HEBREWS 8:12

REFLECTION

The English poet Alexander Pope is crediting with saying, "To err is human; to forgive, divine." Think of a time when you received forgiveness from a friend. Did you have to ask for it? Or was it offered before you could even apologize? How did that person's forgiveness make you feel?

SITUATION

In Hebrews 5 and 7, the writer introduced a man named Melchizedek, a mysterious Old Testament king and priest who offered a blessing to Abraham (see Genesis 14:13–20). The author of Hebrews notes that Melchizedek's priesthood offers a clue for how God was planning on revealing his broader plan of redemption for the world. Melchizedek served as a "type" or foreshadowing of Christ, who now serves as our ultimate high priest—not in an earthly temple but in the "true tabernacle set up by the Lord" in heaven (8:2). Jesus is now the central focus of God's covenant-agreement with his people—and it is a far better covenant than even the great agreement that God established with Abraham and his descendants.

OBSERVATION

*Read Hebrews 8:1–13 from the New International
Version or the New King James Version.*

New International Version

[1] Now the main point of what we are saying is this: We do have such a high priest, who sat down at the right hand of the throne of the Majesty in heaven, [2] and who serves in the sanctuary, the true tabernacle set up by the Lord, not by a mere human being.

[3] Every high priest is appointed to offer both gifts and sacrifices, and so it was necessary for this one also to have something to offer. [4] If he were on earth, he would not be a priest, for there are already priests who offer the gifts prescribed by the law. [5] They serve at a sanctuary that is a copy and shadow of what is in heaven. This is why Moses was warned when he was about to build the tabernacle: "See to it that you make everything according to the pattern shown you on the mountain." [6] But in fact the ministry Jesus has received is as superior to theirs as the covenant of which he is mediator is superior to the old one, since the new covenant is established on better promises.

[7] For if there had been nothing wrong with that first covenant, no place would have been sought for another. [8] But God found fault with the people and said:

> "The days are coming, declares the Lord,
>   when I will make a new covenant
> with the people of Israel
>   and with the people of Judah.
> [9] It will not be like the covenant
>   I made with their ancestors
> when I took them by the hand
>   to lead them out of Egypt,
> because they did not remain faithful to my covenant,

and I turned away from them,
    declares the Lord.
[10] This is the covenant I will establish with the people of Israel
    after that time, declares the Lord.
I will put my laws in their minds
    and write them on their hearts.
I will be their God,
    and they will be my people.
[11] No longer will they teach their neighbor,
    or say to one another, 'Know the Lord,'
because they will all know me,
    from the least of them to the greatest.
[12] For I will forgive their wickedness
    and will remember their sins no more."

[13] By calling this covenant "new," he has made the first one obsolete; and what is obsolete and outdated will soon disappear.

NEW KING JAMES VERSION

[1] Now this is the main point of the things we are saying: We have such a High Priest, who is seated at the right hand of the throne of the Majesty in the heavens, [2] a Minister of the sanctuary and of the true tabernacle which the Lord erected, and not man.

[3] For every high priest is appointed to offer both gifts and sacrifices. Therefore it is necessary that this One also have something to offer. [4] For if He were on earth, He would not be a priest, since there are priests who offer the gifts according to the law; [5] who serve the copy and shadow of the heavenly things, as Moses was divinely instructed when he was about to make the tabernacle. For He said, "See that you make all things according to the pattern shown you on the mountain." [6] But now He has obtained a more excellent ministry, inasmuch as He is also Mediator of a better covenant, which was established on better promises.

[7] For if that first covenant had been faultless, then no place would have been sought for a second. [8] Because finding fault with them, He says: "Behold, the days are coming, says the Lord, when I will make a new covenant with the house of Israel and with the house of Judah— [9] not according to the covenant that I made with their fathers in the day when I took them by the hand to lead them out of the land of Egypt; because they did not continue in My covenant, and I disregarded them, says the Lord. [10] For this is the covenant that I will make with the house of Israel after those days, says the Lord: I will put My laws in their mind and write them on their hearts; and I will be their God, and they shall be My people. [11] None of them shall teach his neighbor, and none his brother, saying, 'Know the Lord,' for all shall know Me, from the least of them to the greatest of them. [12] For I will be merciful to their unrighteousness, and their sins and their lawless deeds I will remember no more."

[13] In that He says, "A new covenant," He has made the first obsolete. Now what is becoming obsolete and growing old is ready to vanish away.

EXPLORATION

1. What are Jesus' duties as high priest in the "true tabernacle set up by the Lord" (verse 2)? How does he fulfill those duties?

_____

_____

_____

_____

2. What does the writer mean when he says the sanctuary in which the Jewish people worshiped on earth was just a "copy and shadow of what is in heaven" (verse 5)?

_____

_____

_____

_____

3. Why is Jesus' priestly work greater than the work of any other priest on earth?

4. How is the new covenant different from the old covenant?

5. Why did God establish a new agreement with his people?

6. What expanded promises did God make to his people under the new covenant?

INSPIRATION

I was thanking the Father today for his mercy. I began listing the sins he'd forgiven. One by one I thanked God for forgiving my stumbles and tumbles. My motives were pure and my heart was thankful, but my understanding of God was wrong. It was when I used the word *remember* that it hit me.

"Remember the time I . . ." I was about to thank God for another act of mercy. But I stopped. Something was wrong. The word *remember* seemed displaced. It was an off-key note in a sonata, a misspelled word in a poem. It was a baseball game in December. It didn't fit. "Does he remember?"

Then I remembered. I remembered his words. "For I will forgive their wickedness and will remember their sins no more" (Hebrews 8:12).

Wow! Now, *that* is a remarkable promise. God doesn't just forgive, he forgets. He erases the board. He destroys the evidence. He clears the computer. . . .

No, he doesn't remember. But I do, you do. You still remember. You're like me. You still remember what you did before you changed. In the cellar of your heart lurk the ghosts of yesterday's sins. Sins you've confessed; errors of which you've repented; damage you've done your best to repair.

And though you're a different person, the ghosts still linger. Though you've locked the basement door, they still haunt you. They float to meet you, spooking your soul and robbing your joy. With wordless whispers they remind you of moments when you forgot whose child you were. . . .

Poltergeists from yesterday's pitfalls. Spiteful specters that slyly suggest, "Are you really forgiven? Sure, God forgets most of our mistakes, but do you think he could actually forget the time you . . ."

Was God exaggerating when he said he would cast our sins as far as the east is from the west? Do you actually believe he would make a statement like "I will not hold their iniquities against them" and then rub our noses in them whenever we ask for help? . . .

You see, God is either the God of perfect grace . . . or he is not God. Grace forgets. Period. He who is perfect love cannot hold grudges. If he does, then he isn't perfect love. And if he isn't perfect love, you might as well put this book down and go fishing, because both of us are chasing fairy tales.

But I believe in his loving forgetfulness. And I believe he has a graciously terrible memory. (From *God Came Near* by Max Lucado.)

REACTION

7. How do you wrap your mind around the fact that God chooses to **forget** your sins when you repent and ask for forgiveness?

_____

_____

_____

8. What do you usually expect when you ask a friend for forgiveness? What can you expect from God when you confess your sins to him?

_____

_____

_____

9. What are some way to remind yourself that God does not hold your sin against you?

_____

_____

_____

10. Why is it tempting to sometimes doubt God's forgiveness?

_____

_____

_____

11. How can you find freedom from a false sense of guilt?

12. Why is it important to express your thanks to God for his forgiveness?

LIFE LESSONS

God not only shows himself willing to forgive and forget, but he also goes out of his way to extend the opportunity for confession and relationship. His covenant gives us permission to count on him. He is determined to fashion a people with whom he will spend eternity—and no obstacle will prevent his plan. All the difficulties that must be overcome and all the hard work that must be done he has done for us. And when we fall and seek his forgiveness, he will restore us and hold none of it against us. We have his word: "I will remember no more."

DEVOTION

Father, thank you for your forgiveness and your gracious forgetfulness. Teach us to confess our sins quickly, to fully accept your forgiveness so we can enjoy a restored relationship with you, and to release any feelings of guilt or self-condemnation. May we experience the joy and freedom that your forgiveness brings.

JOURNALING

What past sins haunt you? How will you forgive yourself for the sins God has already forgiven?

_____

_____

_____

_____

_____

_____

_____

_____

_____

_____

_____

_____

_____

_____

_____

_____

_____

_____

FOR FURTHER READING

To complete the book of Hebrews during this twelve-part study, read Hebrews 8:1–13. For more Bible passages about God's forgiveness, read Numbers 14:18–20; 2 Chronicles 7:14; Nehemiah 9:17; Psalm 86:5; Micah 7:18; Matthew 6:12–14; Mark 2:5–12; and 1 John 1:9.

THE ULTIMATE SACRIFICE

As it is appointed for men to die once, but after this the judgment, so Christ was offered once to bear the sins of many. To those who eagerly wait for Him He will appear a second time, apart from sin, for salvation.

HEBREWS 9:27–28 NKJV

REFLECTION

Imagine being at the scene of Jesus' crucifixion. Consider for a few moments exactly how you picture Jesus on the cross. Now think about your own point of observation. Where are you standing? Near? Far? Are you looking down or up at him? How does your point of view affect the way you respond? What does his suffering for you make you feel?

SITUATION

The author of Hebrews repeatedly sends his Jewish readers back to the Old Testament to help them understand the new covenant that Jesus has brought. Under the old covenant, the people worshiped in an earthly tabernacle, the priest offered animal sacrifices for their sins on the altar, and God's presence was only accessible in the Most Holy Place behind the curtain. These actions would have to be repeated again and again to atone for the people's sins. But Jesus' superior sacrifice on the cross forever replaced this ritual pattern of sacrifice. Jesus entered the Most Holy Place, and through his perfect sacrifice has "once and for all" brought us the possibility of redemption and eternal life with God (9:12). Only Jesus could offer his sinless life as ransom for our sin, and he is now the mediator of this new covenant on our behalf.

OBSERVATION

Read Hebrews 9:11–28 from the New International Version or the New King James Version.

NEW INTERNATIONAL VERSION

[11] But when Christ came as high priest of the good things that are now already here, he went through the greater and more perfect tabernacle that is not made with human hands, that is to say, is not a part of this creation. [12] He did not enter by means of the blood of goats and calves; but he entered the Most Holy Place once for all by his own blood, thus obtaining eternal redemption. [13] The blood of goats and bulls and the ashes of a heifer sprinkled on those who are ceremonially unclean sanctify them so that they are outwardly clean. [14] How much more, then, will the blood of Christ, who through the eternal Spirit offered himself unblemished to God, cleanse our consciences from acts that lead to death, so that we may serve the living God!

[15] For this reason Christ is the mediator of a new covenant, that those who are called may receive the promised eternal inheritance—now that he has died as a ransom to set them free from the sins committed under the first covenant.

[16] In the case of a will, it is necessary to prove the death of the one who made it, [17] because a will is in force only when somebody has died; it never takes effect while the one who made it is living. [18] This is why even the first covenant was not put into effect without blood. [19] When Moses had proclaimed every command of the law to all the people, he took the blood of calves, together with water, scarlet wool and branches of hyssop, and sprinkled the scroll and all the people. [20] He said, "This is the blood of the covenant, which God has commanded you to keep." [21] In the same way, he sprinkled with the blood both the tabernacle and everything used in its ceremonies. [22] In fact, the law requires that nearly everything be cleansed with blood, and without the shedding of blood there is no forgiveness.

²³ It was necessary, then, for the copies of the heavenly things to be purified with these sacrifices, but the heavenly things themselves with better sacrifices than these. ²⁴ For Christ did not enter a sanctuary made with human hands that was only a copy of the true one; he entered heaven itself, now to appear for us in God's presence. ²⁵ Nor did he enter heaven to offer himself again and again, the way the high priest enters the Most Holy Place every year with blood that is not his own. ²⁶ Otherwise Christ would have had to suffer many times since the creation of the world. But he has appeared once for all at the culmination of the ages to do away with sin by the sacrifice of himself. ²⁷ Just as people are destined to die once, and after that to face judgment, ²⁸ so Christ was sacrificed once to take away the sins of many; and he will appear a second time, not to bear sin, but to bring salvation to those who are waiting for him.

NEW KING JAMES VERSION

¹¹ But Christ came as High Priest of the good things to come, with the greater and more perfect tabernacle not made with hands, that is, not of this creation. ¹² Not with the blood of goats and calves, but with His own blood He entered the Most Holy Place once for all, having obtained eternal redemption. ¹³ For if the blood of bulls and goats and the ashes of a heifer, sprinkling the unclean, sanctifies for the purifying of the flesh, ¹⁴ how much more shall the blood of Christ, who through the eternal Spirit offered Himself without spot to God, cleanse your conscience from dead works to serve the living God? ¹⁵ And for this reason He is the Mediator of the new covenant, by means of death, for the redemption of the transgressions under the first covenant, that those who are called may receive the promise of the eternal inheritance.

¹⁶ For where there is a testament, there must also of necessity be the death of the testator. ¹⁷ For a testament is in force after men are dead, since it has no power at all while the testator lives. ¹⁸ Therefore not even the first covenant was dedicated without blood. ¹⁹ For when Moses had spoken every precept to all the people according to the law, he took the blood of calves and goats, with water, scarlet wool, and hyssop,

and sprinkled both the book itself and all the people, [20] saying, "This is the blood of the covenant which God has commanded you." [21] Then likewise he sprinkled with blood both the tabernacle and all the vessels of the ministry. [22] And according to the law almost all things are purified with blood, and without shedding of blood there is no remission.

[23] Therefore it was necessary that the copies of the things in the heavens should be purified with these, but the heavenly things themselves with better sacrifices than these. [24] For Christ has not entered the holy places made with hands, which are copies of the true, but into heaven itself, now to appear in the presence of God for us; [25] not that He should offer Himself often, as the high priest enters the Most Holy Place every year with blood of another— [26] He then would have had to suffer often since the foundation of the world; but now, once at the end of the ages, He has appeared to put away sin by the sacrifice of Himself. [27] And as it is appointed for men to die once, but after this the judgment, [28] so Christ was offered once to bear the sins of many. To those who eagerly wait for Him He will appear a second time, apart from sin, for salvation.

EXPLORATION

1. According to this passage, how did Jesus enter the Most Holy Place?

_____

_____

_____

_____

2. How can people receive the blessings God has promised?

_____

_____

_____

_____

3. Why did Christ establish a new agreement between God and people?

4. Why is the shedding of blood necessary for the forgiveness of sins?

5. How does Christ's blood purify those who accept his sacrifice?

6. How was Christ's sacrifice superior to the sacrifice of animals?

INSPIRATION

Several hundred feet beneath my chair is a lake, an underground cavern of crystalline water known as the Edwards Aquifer. We south-Texans know much about this aquifer. We know its length (175 miles). We know its layout (west to east except under San Antonio, where it runs north to south). We know the water is pure. Fresh. It irrigates farms and waters lawns and fills pools and quenches thirst. We know much about the aquifer.

But for all the facts we do know, there is an essential one we don't. We don't know its size. The depth of the cavern? A mystery. Number of gallons? Unmeasured. . . . "The truth is," a friend told me, "no one knows how much water is down there."

Could this be? I decided to find out. I called a water conservationist. "That's right," he affirmed. "We estimate. We try to measure. But the exact quantity? No one knows." Remarkable. We use it, depend upon it, would perish without it . . . but measure it? We can't.

Bring to mind another unmeasured pool? It might. Not a pool of water but a pool of love. God's love. Aquifer fresh. Pure as April snow. One swallow slackens the thirsty throat and softens the crusty heart. Immerse a life in God's love, and watch it emerge cleansed and changed. We know the impact of God's love.

But the volume? No person has ever measured it.

Moral meteorologists, worried we might exhaust the supply, suggest otherwise. "Don't drink too deeply," they caution, recommending rationed portions. Some people, after all, drink more than their share. Terrorists and traitors and wife beaters—let such scoundrels start drinking, and they may take too much.

But who has plumbed the depths of God's love? Only God has. "Want to see the size of my love?" he invites. "Ascend the winding path outside of Jerusalem. Follow the dots of bloody dirt until you crest the hill. Before looking up, pause and hear me whisper, "This is how much I love you.""

Whip-ripped muscles drape his back. Blood rivulets over his face. His eyes and lips are swollen shut. Pain rages at wildfire intensity. As he sinks to relieve the agony of his legs, his airway closes. At the edge of suffocation, he shoves pierced muscles against the spike and inches up the cross. He does this for hours. Painfully up and down until his strength and our doubts are gone.

Does God love you? Behold the cross, and behold your answer. (From *It's Not About Me* by Max Lucado.)

REACTION

7. Why do people often try to put limits on God's love? What happens as a result?

_____

_____

_____

_____

8. How do people try to make themselves right with God? What results from their efforts?

_____

_____

_____

_____

9. What can free you from the frustration of trying to earn God's approval?

_____

_____

_____

_____

10. What is significant about the fact that Christ died "once for all"?

_____

_____

_____

_____

11. How would you explain to an unbelieving friend why Jesus _had_ to die?

_____

_____

_____

_____

12. How would your life be different if Christ had not died for you?

_____

_____

_____

LIFE LESSONS

Living in a world of choices, it isn't hard for us to assume Jesus is optional. We can easily accept the suggestion that he is one good model among many good models. One great teacher in a long line of great teachers. A godly man, but surely not God. And yet the teaching of Hebrews brings us back to the stark truth. Jesus did something no one else could do, has done, or will do. He struck a bargain with God on our behalf. He served as sacrificial lamb and sacrificing priest. As the God-man, he did what no other human could do. His role for us isn't optional, but essential. We can reject it or accept it. But we dare not consider Jesus only as an option.

DEVOTION

Father, because of your great love for us, you sacrificed your only Son so we could receive forgiveness for our sins and enjoy eternal life with you. We are thankful that you did not hold anything back in your plan to save us. Show us how to give ourselves completely to you in return.

JOURNALING

What benefits and blessings do you enjoy because of Jesus' death on the cross?

_____

_____

_____

_____

_____

_____

_____

_____

_____

_____

_____

_____

FOR FURTHER READING

To complete the book of Hebrews during this twelve-part study, read Hebrews 9:1–28. For more Bible passages about Christ's sacrifice for sin, read John 1:29; Romans 3:22–27; 4:25; 6:23; 2 Corinthians 5:21; 2 Timothy 1:8–10; and 1 John 1:7; 2:2; 4:10.

CONFIDENCE IN CHRIST

So do not throw away your confidence; it will be richly rewarded. You need to persevere so that when you have done the will of God, you will receive what he has promised.

HEBREWS 10:35–36

REFLECTION

Courage and boldness are often traits that are easier to claim than to display. They tend to come out when they are necessary—and not a moment sooner. Think of a time when God gave you courage or boldness. What happened? How did this affect your life?

SITUATION

Up to this point, the writer of Hebrews has focused on teaching, explaining, and inspiring his readers. He has concentrated on explaining the Old Testament rituals and duties of the high priest to highlight the unique work and ministry of Christ. But now he switches gears to offer practical illustrations and applications. He reiterates to his readers that because they have been freed by Jesus' blood and perfect sacrifice, it is time for them to act. It is time for them to step up or step aside. It is time for them—and us—to have confidence in our convictions that Jesus is Lord and then boldly profess this truth to the world.

OBSERVATION

*Read Hebrews 10:19–39 from the New International
Version or the New King James Version.*

NEW INTERNATIONAL VERSION

[19] Therefore, brothers and sisters, since we have confidence to enter the Most Holy Place by the blood of Jesus, [20] by a new and living way opened for us through the curtain, that is, his body, [21] and since we have a great priest over the house of God, [22] let us draw near to God with a sincere heart and with the full assurance that faith brings, having our hearts sprinkled to cleanse us from a guilty conscience and having our bodies washed with pure water. [23] Let us hold unswervingly to the hope we profess, for he who promised is faithful. [24] And let us consider how we may spur one another on toward love and good deeds, [25] not giving up meeting together, as some are in the habit of doing, but encouraging one another—and all the more as you see the Day approaching.

[26] If we deliberately keep on sinning after we have received the knowledge of the truth, no sacrifice for sins is left, [27] but only a fearful expectation of judgment and of raging fire that will consume the enemies of God. [28] Anyone who rejected the law of Moses died without mercy on the testimony of two or three witnesses. [29] How much more severely do you think someone deserves to be punished who has trampled the Son of God underfoot, who has treated as an unholy thing the blood of the covenant that sanctified them, and who has insulted the Spirit of grace? [30] For we know him who said, "It is mine to avenge; I will repay," and again, "The Lord will judge his people." [31] It is a dreadful thing to fall into the hands of the living God.

[32] Remember those earlier days after you had received the light, when you endured in a great conflict full of suffering. [33] Sometimes you were publicly exposed to insult and persecution; at other times you stood side by side with those who were so treated. [34] You suffered along with those in prison and joyfully accepted the confiscation of your property,

because you knew that you yourselves had better and lasting possessions.
³⁵ So do not throw away your confidence; it will be richly rewarded.

³⁶ You need to persevere so that when you have done the will of God,
you will receive what he has promised. ³⁷ For,

> "In just a little while,
> he who is coming will come
> and will not delay."

³⁸ And,

> "But my righteous one will live by faith.
> And I take no pleasure
> in the one who shrinks back."

³⁹ But we do not belong to those who shrink back and are destroyed,
but to those who have faith and are saved.

New King James Version

¹⁹ Therefore, brethren, having boldness to enter the Holiest by the blood
of Jesus, ²⁰ by a new and living way which He consecrated for us, through
the veil, that is, His flesh, ²¹ and having a High Priest over the house
of God, ²² let us draw near with a true heart in full assurance of faith,
having our hearts sprinkled from an evil conscience and our bodies
washed with pure water. ²³ Let us hold fast the confession of our hope
without wavering, for He who promised is faithful. ²⁴ And let us consider
one another in order to stir up love and good works, ²⁵ not forsaking the
assembling of ourselves together, as is the manner of some, but exhorting
one another, and so much the more as you see the Day approaching.

²⁶ For if we sin willfully after we have received the knowledge of the
truth, there no longer remains a sacrifice for sins, ²⁷ but a certain fearful
expectation of judgment, and fiery indignation which will devour the
adversaries. ²⁸ Anyone who has rejected Moses' law dies without mercy

on the testimony of two or three witnesses. [29] Of how much worse punishment, do you suppose, will he be thought worthy who has trampled the Son of God underfoot, counted the blood of the covenant by which he was sanctified a common thing, and insulted the Spirit of grace? [30] For we know Him who said, "Vengeance is Mine, I will repay," says the Lord. And again, "The Lord will judge His people." [31] It is a fearful thing to fall into the hands of the living God.

[32] But recall the former days in which, after you were illuminated, you endured a great struggle with sufferings: [33] partly while you were made a spectacle both by reproaches and tribulations, and partly while you became companions of those who were so treated; [34] for you had compassion on me in my chains, and joyfully accepted the plundering of your goods, knowing that you have a better and an enduring possession for yourselves in heaven. [35] Therefore do not cast away your confidence, which has great reward. [36] For you have need of endurance, so that after you have done the will of God, you may receive the promise:

[37] "For yet a little while,
And He who is coming will come and will not tarry.
[38] Now the just shall live by faith;
But if anyone draws back,
My soul has no pleasure in him."

[39] But we are not of those who draw back to perdition, but of those who believe to the saving of the soul.

EXPLORATION

1. What gives believers in Christ the confidence to approach a holy God?

2. What is the importance of meeting with other believers?

3. What happens when people reject God's salvation and keep on sinning?

4. What warnings does this passage give to people who turn away from their faith in Jesus?

5. What does the author mean when he warns not to "trample the Son of God underfoot" or "insult the Spirit of grace" (verse 29)?

6. Why is it important for believers to not "shirk back" in their faith (verse 39)?

_____

_____

_____

_____

INSPIRATION

Day after day, hour after hour. Relentless, tireless. The Accuser makes a career out of accusing. Unlike the conviction of the Holy Spirit, Satan's condemnation brings no repentance or resolve, just regret. He has one aim: "the thief comes only to steal and kill and destroy" (John 10:10). Steal your peace, kill your dreams, and destroy your future. . . .

But he will not have the last word. Jesus has acted on your behalf.

He stooped. Low enough to sleep in a manger, work in a carpentry shop, sleep in a fishing boat. Low enough to rub shoulders with crooks and lepers. Low enough to be spat upon, slapped, nailed, and speared. Low. Low enough to be buried.

And then he stood. Up from the slab of death. Upright in Joseph's tomb and right in Satan's face. Tall. High. He stood up for the woman and silenced her accusers, and he does the same for you.

"Christ Jesus who died—more than that, who was raised to life—is at the right hand of God and is also interceding for us" (Romans 8:34). Let this sink in for a moment. In the presence of God, in defiance of Satan, Jesus Christ rises to your defense. He takes on the role of a priest. "Since we have a great priest over the house of God, let us draw near to God with a sincere heart and with the full assurance that faith brings, having our hearts sprinkled to cleanse us from a guilty conscience and having our bodies washed with pure water" (Hebrews 10:21–22).

A clean conscience. A clean record. A clean heart. Free from accusation. Free from condemnation. Not just for our past mistakes but also for our future ones. (From *Grace* by Max Lucado.)

REACTION

7. How has Jesus thwarted the plans of the enemy? How has he provided "the last word"?

_____

_____

_____

8. How does the fact that Jesus is standing up for you before God affect your courage?

_____

_____

_____

_____

9. How should your confidence in Christ's ultimate victory change the way you live?

_____

_____

_____

10. How can you help other believers in Christ to show love and do good deeds?

_____

_____

_____

_____

11. What can you gain from remembering the days when you were new in the faith?

_____

_____

_____

_____

12. How can you depend more on other believers to help you grow in your faith and commitment to God?

_____

_____

_____

LIFE LESSONS

Confidence flows out of our intimacy with and sure knowledge of Christ. We are to "enter" and "draw near" because we know Christ's love, because we know what he has done, and because those facts are sinking deeper and deeper into us. We practice boldness when we consider how to "stir up love and good works" in others. We grow in confidence when we persist in spending time with other believers, encouraging them and accepting their encouragement. We have to go beyond knowing the "just live by faith" all the way to living by faith ourselves.

DEVOTION

Father, rekindle the fire that burned bright in our hearts when we first discovered your love and forgiveness. Renew our commitment to you and your work. Help us to be busy about the right business—the business of serving you.

JOURNALING

Do you still have the enthusiasm you possessed when you first became a Christian? If not, how can you reenergize your devotion to Christ?

_____

_____

_____

_____

_____

_____

_____

_____

_____

_____

_____

_____

_____

_____

_____

_____

_____

FOR FURTHER READING

To complete the book of Hebrews during this twelve-part study, read Hebrews 10:1–39. For more Bible passages about our confidence in Christ's victory over death, read John 16:33; Romans 8:31–37; 1 Corinthians 15:24–26, 54–58; 2 Timothy 1:6–8; 1 Peter 2:9; 1 John 4:4; 5:4; and Revelation 3:21; 12:11; 17:14.

LESSON NINE

FAITH IN GOD'S PROMISES

Now faith is the substance of things hoped for, the evidence of things not seen. For by it the elders obtained a good testimony.

HEBREWS 11:1–2 NKJV

REFLECTION

We often do not realize the impact that other believers have had on our lives. Think of three people who have taught you the most about how to live by faith. When was a time you were memorably inspired by their faith in God? What was it that inspired you? How?

SITUATION

The author of Hebrews certainly loved the history of the Jewish people, and he appreciated the way God had worked through them in spite of their many shortcomings. In this next portion of his letter, commonly referred to as the "Bible's Hall of Faith," he highlights some of the key figures from Israel's history and shows how they put their faith in God's plan into *action*. Of particular note in his list is Abraham, who followed God's call "to a place he would later receive as his inheritance" (11:8), and whose acts of faith led to the establishment of Israel as a nation. As the author's words brilliantly illustrate, God was working through people's faith down through the centuries to keep his great plan of redemption on track.

OBSERVATION

*Read Hebrews 11:1–16 from the New International
Version or the New King James Version.*

NEW INTERNATIONAL VERSION

[1] Now faith is confidence in what we hope for and assurance about what we do not see. [2] This is what the ancients were commended for.

[3] By faith we understand that the universe was formed at God's command, so that what is seen was not made out of what was visible.

[4] By faith Abel brought God a better offering than Cain did. By faith he was commended as righteous, when God spoke well of his offerings. And by faith Abel still speaks, even though he is dead.

[5] By faith Enoch was taken from this life, so that he did not experience death: "He could not be found, because God had taken him away." For before he was taken, he was commended as one who pleased God. [6] And without faith it is impossible to please God, because anyone who comes to him must believe that he exists and that he rewards those who earnestly seek him.

[7] By faith Noah, when warned about things not yet seen, in holy fear built an ark to save his family. By his faith he condemned the world and became heir of the righteousness that is in keeping with faith.

[8] By faith Abraham, when called to go to a place he would later receive as his inheritance, obeyed and went, even though he did not know where he was going. [9] By faith he made his home in the promised land like a stranger in a foreign country; he lived in tents, as did Isaac and Jacob, who were heirs with him of the same promise. [10] For he was looking forward to the city with foundations, whose architect and builder is God. [11] And by faith even Sarah, who was past childbearing age, was enabled to bear children because she considered him faithful who had made the promise. [12] And so from this one man, and he as good as dead, came descendants as numerous as the stars in the sky and as countless as the sand on the seashore.

¹³ All these people were still living by faith when they died. They did not receive the things promised; they only saw them and welcomed them from a distance, admitting that they were foreigners and strangers on earth. ¹⁴ People who say such things show that they are looking for a country of their own. ¹⁵ If they had been thinking of the country they had left, they would have had opportunity to return. ¹⁶ Instead, they were longing for a better country—a heavenly one. Therefore God is not ashamed to be called their God, for he has prepared a city for them.

NEW KING JAMES VERSION

¹ Now faith is the substance of things hoped for, the evidence of things not seen. ² For by it the elders obtained a good testimony.

³ By faith we understand that the worlds were framed by the word of God, so that the things which are seen were not made of things which are visible.

⁴ By faith Abel offered to God a more excellent sacrifice than Cain, through which he obtained witness that he was righteous, God testifying of his gifts; and through it he being dead still speaks.

⁵ By faith Enoch was taken away so that he did not see death, "and was not found, because God had taken him"; for before he was taken he had this testimony, that he pleased God. ⁶ But without faith it is impossible to please Him, for he who comes to God must believe that He is, and that He is a rewarder of those who diligently seek Him.

⁷ By faith Noah, being divinely warned of things not yet seen, moved with godly fear, prepared an ark for the saving of his household, by which he condemned the world and became heir of the righteousness which is according to faith.

⁸ By faith Abraham obeyed when he was called to go out to the place which he would receive as an inheritance. And he went out, not knowing where he was going. ⁹ By faith he dwelt in the land of promise as in a foreign country, dwelling in tents with Isaac and Jacob, the heirs with him of the same promise; ¹⁰ for he waited for the city which has foundations, whose builder and maker is God.

[11] By faith Sarah herself also received strength to conceive seed, and she bore a child when she was past the age, because she judged Him faithful who had promised. [12] Therefore from one man, and him as good as dead, were born as many as the stars of the sky in multitude—innumerable as the sand which is by the seashore.

[13] These all died in faith, not having received the promises, but having seen them afar off were assured of them, embraced them and confessed that they were strangers and pilgrims on the earth. [14] For those who say such things declare plainly that they seek a homeland. [15] And truly if they had called to mind that country from which they had come out, they would have had opportunity to return. [16] But now they desire a better, that is, a heavenly country. Therefore God is not ashamed to be called their God, for He has prepared a city for them.

EXPLORATION

1. How does the author of Hebrews define *faith* in this passage?

2. Why is it important to remember people of faith who lived in the past?

3. What made the faith of the people in this passage so extraordinary?

4. How did these people demonstrate their faith in God?

_____

_____

_____

_____

5. Why did these people say they were like "foreigners and strangers on earth" (verse 13)?

_____

_____

_____

_____

6. How can God's people today show their trust in his promises?

_____

_____

_____

_____

INSPIRATION

Sitting at the sidewalk cafe table next to yours is a young man, twentyish, dark hair. His dress suggests working class; sinewy muscles and sunned skin imply outdoor work. Lawn maintenance? Carpentry? You don't mean to stare . . . but he has a different look to him. His complexion and facial features tag him as foreign. You don't mean to stare, but before you can stop, he notices and smiles.

"I'm Hebrew."

"Sorry?"

"You're not the first to wonder about me. I'm Hebrew. Only been in Egypt a couple of years."

You shift your chair in his direction and lean forward. "What brought you here?"

"Might I give the short version?" . . .

You nod and he begins.

"Well, my father tricked my uncle out of his inheritance. Of course, Grandma wanted my father to swindle my uncle. She was the brains behind the ploy. Uncle Esau, so angry at being suckered, decided to kill my father. Dad escaped with the shirt on his back and his head on his shoulders and was happy to have that. . . . Plan on finishing that humus?"

You hand him your plate and stare as he spoons it clean and wonder what kind of story this might be. Scoundrels scamming deceivers. Cheats misleading two-timers. What kind of people are these? Exactly the kind who comprise God's cast of characters. Joseph and his family are just a few of the *hoi polloi* and ne'er-do-wells whose stories form the stuff of Scripture. . . .

Story after story marked by scandal, stumble, and intrigue. Who are these people?

Us. That's who they are.

We find our stories in theirs. We find our hope where they found theirs. In the midst of them all . . . hovering over them all . . . is the hero of it all: God. Maker. Shaper. Rescuer of sinking hearts. God. Passing out high callings, second chances, and moral compasses to all comers and takers. To Moses—who murdered; Samson—who slipped; Thomas—who second-guessed God; to John the Baptist—who dressed like a caveman and had the diet of a grizzly bear.

These are the people of the Bible, brimming with much more spunk and spark than many people realize. . . . And if God can find a place for these characters . . . he just might have a place for us too. A jewel of a verse from the book of Hebrews implies as much. "The one who makes people holy and those who are made holy are of the same family. So Jesus is not ashamed to call them his brothers and sisters" (Hebrews 2:11).

The passage has the feel of a family reunion photo. An assemblage of aunts, uncles, cousins, and kin, gathered for a wedding, summer picnic, or holiday. All the curious characters of the family are present. . . .

Do you see your face in the photo? I hope you do . . . you're in it. And he's proud of you too. (From *Cast of Characters* by Max Lucado.)

REACTION

7. None of the people listed in the "Bible's Hall of Faith" were perfect by any means. What does this tell you about the kind of person God can use for his plans?

_____

_____

_____

_____

8. How do faith and obedience work together?

_____

_____

_____

9. Why is it impossible to please God without faith?

_____

_____

_____

10. How does God respond when you choose to act on your faith?

_____

_____

_____

_____

We use casual faith in a thousand ways

11. How has your faith in God changed your perspective or your goals in life?

12. What can you do to exercise your faith in God this week?

LIFE LESSONS

We use casual faith in a thousand ways every day without thinking about it. Every time we sit in a chair, drive a car, or eat a bite of food, we are exercising trust. We can't prove the chair will hold us or the car is safe or the food isn't poisonous. We simply practice *unintentional* faith. But that is not the kind of faith God expects from us. The examples of faith we have seen in this passage in Hebrews show us *intentional* faith—faith that God is there and is active in our lives. This is a faith that doesn't know the immediate outcome but trusts God anyway, that suffers because it knows there's more at stake than the immediate situation, and that doesn't really expect everything to work out on this side of eternity. This is the faith that pleases God.

DEVOTION

Father, our faith can be so weak. Forgive us for doubting you. Help us to persevere even when we haven't seen all of your promises fulfilled. Remind us that we are just passing through this life by focusing our eyes on a better country—our heavenly home.

JOURNALING

What specific things have happened in your life that remind you of God's faithfulness?

_____

_____

_____

_____

_____

_____

_____

_____

_____

_____

_____

_____

_____

_____

_____

_____

_____

FOR FURTHER READING

To complete the book of Hebrews during this twelve-part study, read Hebrews 11:1–40. For more Bible passages about faith, read 2 Chronicles 20:20; Matthew 21:21–22; Acts 15:8–9; Romans 5:1–2; 1 Corinthians 16:13; Galatians 2:15–16; 3:22–27; James 2:14–26; 1 Peter 1:8–9; and Jude 1:3, 20.

LESSON TEN

SUFFERING SERVES
A PURPOSE

No discipline seems pleasant at the time, but painful.
Later on, however, it produces a harvest of righteousness
and peace for those who have been trained by it.
HEBREWS 12:11

REFLECTION

Good coaches explain their expectations and allow their players to learn from their mistakes. The same is true in life. The most valuable lessons we learn are often remembered by the pain we suffered in learning them! Think of a time when you endured something painful because you knew it would ultimately benefit you. What was your experience? How did you benefit?

SITUATION

The author of Hebrews began his inspiring roll call of the great people of the faith with Abel (see 11:4) and ended with David, Samuel, the prophets, and unnamed others (see 11:32–37). In this next section, he moves the spotlight from these heroes of the Jewish faith onto his readers, who must now follow in their ancestors' footsteps and "run the race" marked out for them. As they do this, they need to focus on a name that he has not yet mentioned in his list—a name that is above all other names. Jesus, the author notes, is the "pioneer and perfecter" of their faith (12:2), and he is their ultimate example of how to persevere in spite of suffering.

OBSERVATION

Read Hebrews 12:1–11 from the New International
Version or the New King James Version.

NEW INTERNATIONAL VERSION
[1] Therefore, since we are surrounded by such a great cloud of witnesses, let us throw off everything that hinders and the sin that so easily entangles. And let us run with perseverance the race marked out for us, [2] fixing our eyes on Jesus, the pioneer and perfecter of faith. For the joy set before him he endured the cross, scorning its shame, and sat down at the right hand of the throne of God. [3] Consider him who endured such opposition from sinners, so that you will not grow weary and lose heart.

[4] In your struggle against sin, you have not yet resisted to the point of shedding your blood. [5] And have you completely forgotten this word of encouragement that addresses you as a father addresses his son? It says,

> "My son, do not make light of the Lord's discipline,
>   and do not lose heart when he rebukes you,
> [6] because the Lord disciplines the one he loves,
>   and he chastens everyone he accepts as his son."

[7] Endure hardship as discipline; God is treating you as his children. For what children are not disciplined by their father? [8] If you are not disciplined—and everyone undergoes discipline—then you are not legitimate, not true sons and daughters at all. [9] Moreover, we have all had human fathers who disciplined us and we respected them for it. How much more should we submit to the Father of spirits and live!

¹⁰ They disciplined us for a little while as they thought best; but God disciplines us for our good, in order that we may share in his holiness. ¹¹ No discipline seems pleasant at the time, but painful. Later on, however, it produces a harvest of righteousness and peace for those who have been trained by it.

New King James Version

¹ Therefore we also, since we are surrounded by so great a cloud of witnesses, let us lay aside every weight, and the sin which so easily ensnares us, and let us run with endurance the race that is set before us, ² looking unto Jesus, the author and finisher of our faith, who for the joy that was set before Him endured the cross, despising the shame, and has sat down at the right hand of the throne of God.

³ For consider Him who endured such hostility from sinners against Himself, lest you become weary and discouraged in your souls. ⁴ You have not yet resisted to bloodshed, striving against sin. ⁵ And you have forgotten the exhortation which speaks to you as to sons:

"My son, do not despise the chastening of the Lord,
Nor be discouraged when you are rebuked by Him;
⁶ For whom the Lord loves He chastens,
And scourges every son whom He receives."

⁷ If you endure chastening, God deals with you as with sons; for what son is there whom a father does not chasten? ⁸ But if you are without chastening, of which all have become partakers, then you are illegitimate and not sons. ⁹ Furthermore, we have had human fathers who corrected us, and we paid them respect. Shall we not much more readily be in subjection to the Father of spirits and live? ¹⁰ For they indeed for a few days chastened us as seemed best to them, but He for our profit, that we may be partakers of His holiness. ¹¹ Now no chastening seems to be joyful for the present, but painful; nevertheless, afterward it yields the peaceable fruit of righteousness to those who have been trained by it.

EXPLORATION

1. What does it mean that Jesus is the "pioneer and perfecter" of your faith (verse 2)?

2. Why did Jesus accept the shame of the cross?

3. What advice does this passage offer to those who are suffering?

4. Whom does God discipline? How does suffering fit in?

5. What are some reasons this passages offers as to why God allows his children to suffer?

6. Think about the difference between discipline as *punishment* and discipline as *training*. Why is it important to accept God's discipline if you want to grow in spiritual maturity?

_____

_____

_____

_____

INSPIRATION

He looked around the carpentry shop. He stood for a moment in the refuge of the little room that housed so many sweet memories. He balanced the hammer in his hand. He ran his fingers across the sharp teeth of the saw. He stroked the smoothly worn wood of the sawhorse. He had come to say goodbye.

It was time for him to leave. He had heard something that made him know it was time to go. So he came one last time to smell the sawdust and lumber.

Life was peaceful here. Life was so . . . safe . . .

I wonder if he wanted to stay. "I could do a good job here in Nazareth. Settle down. Raise a family. Be a civic leader."

I wonder because I know he had already read the last chapter. He knew that the feet that would step out of the safe shadow of the carpentry shop would not rest until they'd been pierced and placed on a Roman cross. . . .

If there was any hesitation on the part of his humanity, it was overcome by the compassion of his divinity. His divinity heard the voices . . . And his divinity saw the faces . . . From the face of Adam to the face of the infant born somewhere in the world as you read these words, he saw them all.

And you can be sure of one thing. Among the voices that found their way into that carpentry shop in Nazareth was your voice. . . . Not only did he hear you; he saw you. He saw your face aglow the hour you first knew him. He saw your face in shame the hour you first fell. The same face that looked back at you from this morning's mirror, looked at him. And it was enough to kill him.

He left because of you.

He laid his security down with his hammer. He hung tranquility on the peg with his nail apron. He closed the window shutters on the sunshine of his youth and locked the door on the comfort and ease of anonymity.

Since he could bear your sins more easily than he could bear the thought of your hopelessness, he chose to leave. It wasn't easy. Leaving the carpentry shop never has been. (From *God Came Near* by Max Lucado.)

REACTION

7. What does Jesus' example show about why it is important to follow God's will . . . even if that requires suffering at times?

8. Read Romans 8:15. How does God see you? Why does he discipline you at times?

9. How can you learn to recognize and respond to God's correction in your life?

10. How does this passage challenge your attitude toward God's discipline?

_____

_____

_____

_____

11. What might God be teaching you through some present difficulties?

_____

_____

_____

12. Why is it important to remember that God loves you even though he disciplines you?

_____

_____

_____

LIFE LESSONS

We often miss the best lessons and benefits of discipline because we insist on thinking of it primarily as punishment rather than training. We fail to see God's purposes in the "race set before us," so we don't approach it in the way Jesus approached the "joy set before him." One of the best exercises to break out of the resentment habit when it comes to discipline is to take a different tack: question the good stuff. It's easy to question pain and suffering. But how often do we question God's continual blessings, goodness, mercy, and kindness? How often do we say, "Why did I have such a good day today?" or "Lord, why did you supply that need today?" God has a purpose in everything that comes our way, whether it's suffering or grace.

DEVOTION

Father, forgive us for the times we have shaken our heads and pounded our fists against the earth and cried, "Why, God?" For Father, we know that when you allow us to suffer, you have our best interests at heart. Teach us to submit to your will instead of fighting for our own way. And in our darkest moments, remind us that you still love us.

JOURNALING

How has God's discipline improved your life and made you a more mature believer?

FOR FURTHER READING

To complete the book of Hebrews during this twelve-part study, read Hebrews 12:1–11. For more Bible passages about God's discipline, read Deuteronomy 4:36; 11:2–7; Job 5:17; Psalm 94:12; Proverbs 3:11; 10:17; Jeremiah 30:11; Hosea 5:1–2; and Revelation 3:19.

THE FEAR
OF THE LORD

*Therefore, since we are receiving a kingdom which
cannot be shaken, let us have grace, by which we
may serve God acceptably with reverence and
godly fear. For our God is a consuming fire.*
HEBREWS 12:28–29 NKJV

REFLECTION

Think of a person you greatly admire. Do you find it easy to talk with that person, or do you just admire him or her from a distance? Would you be nervous or thrilled if that person approached you? How do you show your respect for that individual?

SITUATION

As the writer of Hebrews notes, Jesus was willing to endure the shame and suffering of the cross to fulfill his Father's purpose. For this reason, Christ's example should serve as our ultimate motivation for enduring in our faith and not growing weary in pursuing God's will. While our heavenly Father will discipline us at times, we can know this is intended to produce a "harvest of righteousness" that is for our benefit (12:11). Following hard on the heels of this teaching, the author now urges us to live out what we know. He draws on the Old Testament imagery of God appearing to his people on Mount Sinai to show his readers—and us—that we serve an awesome God and are headed to an awesome heavenly city.

OBSERVATION

Read Hebrews 12:12–29 from the New International
Version or the New King James Version.

NEW INTERNATIONAL VERSION

[12] Therefore, strengthen your feeble arms and weak knees. [13] "Make level paths for your feet," so that the lame may not be disabled, but rather healed.

[14] Make every effort to live in peace with everyone and to be holy; without holiness no one will see the Lord. [15] See to it that no one falls short of the grace of God and that no bitter root grows up to cause trouble and defile many. [16] See that no one is sexually immoral, or is godless like Esau, who for a single meal sold his inheritance rights as the oldest son. [17] Afterward, as you know, when he wanted to inherit this blessing, he was rejected. Even though he sought the blessing with tears, he could not change what he had done.

[18] You have not come to a mountain that can be touched and that is burning with fire; to darkness, gloom and storm; [19] to a trumpet blast or to such a voice speaking words that those who heard it begged that no further word be spoken to them, [20] because they could not bear what was commanded: "If even an animal touches the mountain, it must be stoned to death." [21] The sight was so terrifying that Moses said, "I am trembling with fear."

[22] But you have come to Mount Zion, to the city of the living God, the heavenly Jerusalem. You have come to thousands upon thousands of angels in joyful assembly, [23] to the church of the firstborn, whose names are written in heaven. You have come to God, the Judge of all, to the spirits of the righteous made perfect, [24] to Jesus the mediator of a new covenant, and to the sprinkled blood that speaks a better word than the blood of Abel.

[25] See to it that you do not refuse him who speaks. If they did not escape when they refused him who warned them on earth, how much

less will we, if we turn away from him who warns us from heaven? [26] At that time his voice shook the earth, but now he has promised, "Once more I will shake not only the earth but also the heavens." [27] The words "once more" indicate the removing of what can be shaken—that is, created things—so that what cannot be shaken may remain.

[28] Therefore, since we are receiving a kingdom that cannot be shaken, let us be thankful, and so worship God acceptably with reverence and awe, [29] for our "God is a consuming fire."

NEW KING JAMES VERSION

[12] Therefore strengthen the hands which hang down, and the feeble knees, [13] and make straight paths for your feet, so that what is lame may not be dislocated, but rather be healed.

[14] Pursue peace with all people, and holiness, without which no one will see the Lord: [15] looking carefully lest anyone fall short of the grace of God; lest any root of bitterness springing up cause trouble, and by this many become defiled; [16] lest there be any fornicator or profane person like Esau, who for one morsel of food sold his birthright. [17] For you know that afterward, when he wanted to inherit the blessing, he was rejected, for he found no place for repentance, though he sought it diligently with tears.

[18] For you have not come to the mountain that may be touched and that burned with fire, and to blackness and darkness and tempest, [19] and the sound of a trumpet and the voice of words, so that those who heard it begged that the word should not be spoken to them anymore. [20] (For they could not endure what was commanded: "And if so much as a beast touches the mountain, it shall be stoned or shot with an arrow." [21] And so terrifying was the sight that Moses said, "I am exceedingly afraid and trembling.")

[22] But you have come to Mount Zion and to the city of the living God, the heavenly Jerusalem, to an innumerable company of angels, [23] to the general assembly and church of the firstborn who are registered in heaven, to God the Judge of all, to the spirits of just men made

perfect, [24] to Jesus the Mediator of the new covenant, and to the blood of sprinkling that speaks better things than that of Abel.

[25] See that you do not refuse Him who speaks. For if they did not escape who refused Him who spoke on earth, much more shall we not escape if we turn away from Him who speaks from heaven, [26] whose voice then shook the earth; but now He has promised, saying, "Yet once more I shake not only the earth, but also heaven." [27] Now this, "Yet once more," indicates the removal of those things that are being shaken, as of things that are made, that the things which cannot be shaken may remain.

[28] Therefore, since we are receiving a kingdom which cannot be shaken, let us have grace, by which we may serve God acceptably with reverence and godly fear. [29] For our God is a consuming fire.

EXPLORATION

1. Why should believers "live in peace with everyone" and "be holy" (verse 14)?

_____

_____

_____

_____

_____

2. Read Genesis 25:29–34. How can Christians avoid making the mistake that Esau made?

_____

_____

_____

_____

3. How did the people of the Old Testament relate to God? What does the author of Hebrews say has changed in the way we can relate to God?

_____

_____

_____

4. What does the author say believers enter into when they decide to follow Christ?

_____

_____

_____

5. What will remain after God destroys this world?

_____

_____

_____

6. What kind of worship pleases God?

_____

_____

_____

INSPIRATION

When you list the claims that qualify Jesus as either crazy or kingly, don't omit this one: he asserted to have the only sinless heart in all of history. . . . Jesus' standard mutes all boasting.

I experienced a remotely similar standard when I met golf legend Byron Nelson. Brand-new to the game, I had just broken a hundred on the golf course for the first time. A friend had an appointment with Mr. Nelson and asked me to come along. En route I bragged about my double-digit score, offering a hole-by-hole summary. Fearing I might do the same with the retired icon, my friend asked what I knew of Byron Nelson's accomplishments, and then he told me. . . . My score of ninety-eight seemed suddenly insignificant.

Mr. Nelson's standard silenced me. Jesus' perfection silences us.

So how does he respond to our unholy hearts? Can a good cardiologist spot irregularity and dismiss it? Can God overlook our sins as innocent mistakes? No. He is the one and only judge. He issues decrees, not opinions; commands, not suggestions. They are truth. They emerge from his holy self. Violate them, and you dethrone him—dethrone him at the highest cost.

Jesus made his position clear: "Without holiness no one will see the Lord" (Hebrews 12:14). Hard-hearted souls will not populate heaven. . . .

Though healthy, Jesus took our disease upon himself. Though diseased, we who accept his offer are pronounced healthy. More than pardoned, we are declared innocent. We enter heaven, not with healed hearts, but with his heart. It is as if we have never sinned. . . .

This is no transplant, mind you, but a swap. The holy and the vile exchange locations. God makes healthy what was sick, right what was wrong, straight what was crooked. (From *3:16: The Numbers of Hope* by Max Lucado.)

REACTION

7. What does the author of Hebrews say is required for you to see the Lord?

_____

_____

_____

_____

8. What did Jesus do to allow you to have access to a holy God?

9. What does it mean to "fear" God?

10. How does the fear of the Lord affect your daily life?

11. This world will one day be "shaken" and removed. Given this, how should you spend our time and energy while you are here on earth?

12. What does the way you spend your time reveal about your view of God?

LIFE LESSONS

God, who came to us in Christ, is certainly worthy to be feared—as in literally provoking terror. But he welcomes us to approach him in another kind of fear: awe, honor, respect, and trust. Our capacity to appreciate what God has done in us and what he will do through us always flows from our fear of God. Fearing God leads to serving him. The *how* of doing God's will comes through our continual exposure to God's Word and God's Spirit. The *what* of doing God's will comes mostly from within, recognizing the way God has put us together, and trusting his purposes in how we are wired.

DEVOTION

Heavenly Father, teach us what it means to worship you in reverence and awe. Purify us and make us holy as we eagerly wait for your unshakable kingdom to come to earth. Help us to see what is important, what is eternal, and what is lasting.

JOURNALING

How can you demonstrate your reverence for God today?

FOR FURTHER READING

To complete the book of Hebrews during this twelve-part study, read Hebrews 12:12–29. For more Bible passages about fearing God, read Deuteronomy 31:12–13; 1 Samuel 12:14–15; Psalms 2:11; 19:9; 147:11; Proverbs 1:7; Isaiah 33:6; Luke 12:5; and 2 Corinthians 5:11.

LESSON TWELVE

SERVING OTHERS

Do not forget to show hospitality to strangers,
for by so doing some people have shown
hospitality to angels without knowing it.
HEBREWS 13:2

REFLECTION

Jesus described his purpose for coming to earth as being one of *service.* He told his disciples, "The Son of Man did not come to be served, but to serve, and to give his life as a ransom for many" (Matthew 30:28). When has a Christian brother or sister served you in a meaningful way? How did this act of service affect you?

SITUATION

The writer of Hebrews has explored a number of important themes in his letter. He has demonstrated to his Jewish readers how Jesus and the new covenant he brought is superior to everything under that was under the old covenant—and why they should thus not doubt their decision to put their faith in Christ. The author now devotes his closing words to a theme he has touched on repeatedly throughout the letter: *love* and *service.* He offers a fervent appeal for his readers to not be carried away "by all kinds of strange teachings" (13:9), to cling to the superior sacrifice Jesus has offered for them, and to see every relationship and every situation as an opportunity to *serve* others in love in the name of Christ.

OBSERVATION

*Read Hebrews 13:1–16 from the New International
Version or the New King James Version.*

New International Version

¹ Keep on loving one another as brothers and sisters. ² Do not forget to show hospitality to strangers, for by so doing some people have shown hospitality to angels without knowing it. ³ Continue to remember those in prison as if you were together with them in prison, and those who are mistreated as if you yourselves were suffering.

⁴ Marriage should be honored by all, and the marriage bed kept pure, for God will judge the adulterer and all the sexually immoral. ⁵ Keep your lives free from the love of money and be content with what you have, because God has said,

> "Never will I leave you;
> never will I forsake you."

⁶ So we say with confidence,

> "The Lord is my helper; I will not be afraid.
> What can mere mortals do to me?"

⁷ Remember your leaders, who spoke the word of God to you. Consider the outcome of their way of life and imitate their faith. ⁸ Jesus Christ is the same yesterday and today and forever.

⁹ Do not be carried away by all kinds of strange teachings. It is good for our hearts to be strengthened by grace, not by eating ceremonial foods, which is of no benefit to those who do so. ¹⁰ We have an altar from which those who minister at the tabernacle have no right to eat.

¹¹ The high priest carries the blood of animals into the Most Holy Place as a sin offering, but the bodies are burned outside the camp.

¹² And so Jesus also suffered outside the city gate to make the people holy through his own blood. ¹³ Let us, then, go to him outside the camp, bearing the disgrace he bore. ¹⁴ For here we do not have an enduring city, but we are looking for the city that is to come.

¹⁵ Through Jesus, therefore, let us continually offer to God a sacrifice of praise—the fruit of lips that openly profess his name. ¹⁶ And do not forget to do good and to share with others, for with such sacrifices God is pleased.

NEW KING JAMES VERSION

¹ Let brotherly love continue. ² Do not forget to entertain strangers, for by so doing some have unwittingly entertained angels. ³ Remember the prisoners as if chained with them—those who are mistreated—since you yourselves are in the body also.

⁴ Marriage is honorable among all, and the bed undefiled; but fornicators and adulterers God will judge.

⁵ Let your conduct be without covetousness; be content with such things as you have. For He Himself has said, "I will never leave you nor forsake you." ⁶ So we may boldly say:

> "The LORD is my helper;
> I will not fear.
> What can man do to me?"

⁷ Remember those who rule over you, who have spoken the word of God to you, whose faith follow, considering the outcome of their conduct. ⁸ Jesus Christ is the same yesterday, today, and forever. ⁹ Do not be carried about with various and strange doctrines. For it is good that the heart be established by grace, not with foods which have not profited those who have been occupied with them.

¹⁰ We have an altar from which those who serve the tabernacle have no right to eat. ¹¹ For the bodies of those animals, whose blood is brought into the sanctuary by the high priest for sin, are burned outside the

camp. [12] Therefore Jesus also, that He might sanctify the people with His own blood, suffered outside the gate. [13] Therefore let us go forth to Him, outside the camp, bearing His reproach. [14] For here we have no continuing city, but we seek the one to come. [15] Therefore by Him let us continually offer the sacrifice of praise to God, that is, the fruit of our lips, giving thanks to His name. [16] But do not forget to do good and to share, for with such sacrifices God is well pleased.

EXPLORATION

1. How should believers in Christ show their love for one another?

_____

_____

_____

_____

_____

2. What responsibility do believers have to help people in need? Why?

_____

_____

_____

_____

3. How are believers in Christ to regard marriage? How are they to regard money?

_____

_____

_____

_____

4. What does it mean to be carried away by "strange teachings" (verse 9)?

5. What is the future city described in this passage? Why does the author mention it?

6. According to this passage, what kind of sacrifices please God?

INSPIRATION

Two great problems in serving others are both problems of human nature, of focusing on our relationship with people instead of our relationship with Christ. The first problem is that people will expect too much of you; and the second, you will expect too much of them. Both of these problems are problems of unrealistic expectations. Expectations must be focused on Christ, not each other. He is the only One who will consistently not let us down.

The milk of human sympathy will undernourish your soul. No amount of human gratitude will properly compensate your effort to improve the human condition. When we focus on serving the person, we are inevitably disappointed. And what's more, we will disappoint them.

Serving people for the sake of their gratitude is a guaranteed formula for disappointment. Just when you begin to feel good about your labors, someone lets you down. Or, more likely, someone will expect too much from you and accuse you of letting them down. Either way, your destiny is to be terribly discouraged. . . .

The key is the personal relationship with Christ. The focus must not be on serving others or on being served. The focus must be on Jesus, on becoming so absorbed in the relationship with Him that every other thing is a response to our relationship. We don't serve men; we serve God. Have no expectations of men. Focus on the personal relationship with Him, and there will be an overflow available for others.

Look to Christ alone for gratitude. If you serve Christ, then you will remember to look to Him for your approval, not to the milk of human sympathy. He will reward you for serving others; in fact, He is the reward . . . The personal relationship with Christ is the oasis in the desert of human relations. When people begin to wear you down, let it remind you that you are not in the overflow. It is time to drink of Christ. (From *Walking with Christ in the Details of Life* by Patrick Morley.)

REACTION

7. How has your relationship with Jesus changed the way you treat others?

_____

_____

_____

_____

8. What problems are likely to arise in serving others?

_____

_____

_____

_____

9. How can you avoid or deal with those problems?

_____

_____

_____

10. What is the key to enjoying Christian service?

_____

_____

_____

11. What can you do when you feel discouraged about your ministry?

_____

_____

_____

12. How can you remind yourself to seek only Christ's approval for your service?

_____

_____

_____

LIFE LESSONS

The author of Hebrews began with a tribute to God's ultimate word spoken in and through Jesus Christ. He ends with a tribute to God's ultimate work in raising the "Lord Jesus from the dead" (13:20 NKJV) and for equipping us "with everything good for doing his will" (verse 21). Throughout the letter, the author has asked us to look back to the Old

Testament—not with the intention of reliving *those* days, but to help us live in *these* days. God filled the history of his people with lessons that illuminate his magnificent plan for all people. Through the words of Hebrews we hear the voices of the ages, urging us to keep the faith in our times.

DEVOTION

Father, thank you for the example of Christ's humble service. Thank you for the people of faith who have gone before us and modelled service. Keep our eyes focused on you and protect us from selfish desires. May your great love for us spur us on to love and serve one another.

JOURNALING

What humble act of service can you offer to God today?

FOR FURTHER READING

To complete the book of Hebrews during this twelve-part study, read Hebrews 13:1–25. For more Bible passages about serving the Lord, read Psalm 2:11; Luke 12:35–40; 1 Corinthians 16:15–16; Galatians 5:13; Ephesians 4:11–13; Colossians 3:23–24; and 1 Timothy 6:2.

LEADER'S GUIDE FOR SMALL GROUPS

Thank you for your willingness to lead a group through *Life Lessons from Hebrews*. The rewards of being a leader are different from those of participating, and we hope you find your own walk with Jesus deepened by this experience. During the twelve lessons in this study, you will guide your group through selected passages in Hebrews and explore the key themes of the letter. There are several elements in this leader's guide that will help you as you structure your study and reflection time, so be sure to follow along and take advantage of each one.

BEFORE YOU BEGIN

Before your first meeting, make sure the group members have their own copy of the *Life Lessons from Hebrews* study guide so they can follow along and have their answers written out ahead of time. Alternately, you can hand out the guides at your first meeting and give the group some time to look over the material and ask any preliminary questions. Be sure to send a sheet around the room during that first meeting and have the members write down their name, phone number, and email address so you can keep in touch with them during the week.

There are several ways to structure the duration of the study. You can choose to cover each lesson individually for a total of twelve weeks of discussion, or you can combine two lessons together per week for a total of six weeks of discussion. You can also choose to have the group members read just the selected passages of Scripture given in each lesson, or they can cover the entire book of Hebrews by reading the material listed in the "For Further Reading" section at the end of each lesson. The following table illustrates these options:

Twelve-Week Format

Week	Lessons Covered	Simplified Reading	Expanded Reading
1	Jesus Understands Us	Hebrews 2:10–18	Hebrews 1:1–2:18
2	Keep the Faith	Hebrews 3:1–14	Hebrews 3:1–19
3	God's Rest	Hebrews 4:1–11	Hebrews 4:1–13
4	Jesus, Our High Priest	Hebrews 4:14–5:10	Hebrews 4:14–5:14
5	Perseverance	Hebrews 6:7–20	Hebrews 6:1–7:28
6	God Forgives and Forgets	Hebrews 8:1–13	Hebrews 8:1–13
7	The Ultimate Sacrifice	Hebrews 9:11–28	Hebrews 9:1–28
8	Confidence in Christ	Hebrews 10:19–39	Hebrews 10:1–39
9	Faith in God's Promises	Hebrews 11:1–16	Hebrews 11:1–40
10	Suffering Serves a Purpose	Hebrews 12:1–11	Hebrews 12:1–11
11	The Fear of the Lord	Hebrews 12:12–29	Hebrews 12:12–29
12	Serving Others	Hebrews 13:1–16	Hebrews 13:1–25

Six-Week Format

Week	Lessons Covered	Simplified Reading	Expanded Reading
1	Jesus Understands Us / Keep the Faith	Hebrews 2:10–3:14	Hebrews 1:1–3:19
2	God's Rest / Jesus, Our High Priest	Hebrews 4:1–11, 14–16; 5:1–5:10	Hebrews 4:1–5:14
3	Perseverance / God Forgives and Forgets	Hebrews 6:7–20; 8:1–13	Hebrews 6:1–8:13
4	The Ultimate Sacrifice / Confidence in Christ	Hebrews 9:11–28; 10:19–39	Hebrews 9:1–10:39
5	Faith in God's Promises / Suffering Serves a Purpose	Hebrews 11:1–16; 12:1–11	Hebrews 11:1–12:11
6	The Fear of the Lord / Serving Others	Hebrews 12:12–13:16	Hebrews 12:12–13:25

Generally, the ideal size you will want for the group is between eight to ten people, which ensures everyone will have enough time to participate in discussions. If you have more people, you might want to break up the main group into smaller subgroups. Encourage those who show up at the first meeting to commit to attending the duration of the study, as this will help the group members get to know each other, create stability for the group, and help you know how to prepare each week.

Each of the lessons begins with a brief reflection that highlights the theme you will be discussing that week. As you begin your group time, have the group members briefly respond to the opening question to get them thinking about the topic at hand. Some people may want to tell a long story in response to one of these questions, but the goal is to keep the answers brief. Ideally, you want everyone in the group to get a chance to answer, so try to keep the responses to just a few minutes. If you have more talkative group members, say up front that everyone needs to limit his or her answer to two minutes.

Give the group members a chance to answer, but tell them to feel free to pass if they wish. With the rest of the study, it's generally not a good idea to have everyone answer every question—a free-flowing discussion is more desirable. But with the opening reflection question, you can go around the circle. Encourage shy people to share, but don't force them.

Before your first meeting, let the group members know how the lessons are broken down. During your group discussion time the members will be drawing on the answers they wrote to the Exploration and Reaction sections, so encourage them to always complete these ahead of time. Also, invite them to bring any questions and insights they uncovered while reading to your next meeting, especially if they had a breakthrough moment or if they didn't understand something they read.

WEEKLY PREPARATION

As the leader, there are a few things you should do to prepare for each meeting:

- *Read through the lesson.* This will help you to become familiar with the content and know how to structure the discussion times.
- *Decide which questions you want to discuss.* Depending on how you structure your group time, you may not be able to cover every question. So select the questions ahead of time that you absolutely want the group to explore.
- *Be familiar with the questions you want to discuss.* When the group meets you'll be watching the clock, so you want to make sure you are familiar with the Bible study questions you have selected. You can then spend time in the passage again when the group meets. In this way, you'll ensure you have the passage more deeply in your mind than your group members.
- *Pray for your group.* Pray for your group members throughout the week and ask God to lead them as they study his Word.
- *Bring extra supplies to your meeting.* The members should bring their own pens for writing notes, but it's a good idea to have extras available for those who forget. You may also want to bring paper and additional Bibles.

Note that in many cases there will not be one "right" answer to the question. Answers will vary, especially when the group members are being asked to share their personal experiences.

STRUCTURING THE DISCUSSION TIME

You will need to determine with your group how long you want to meet each week so you can plan your time accordingly. Generally, most groups like to meet for either sixty minutes or ninety minutes, so you could use one of the following schedules:

Section	60 Minutes	90 Minutes
WELCOME (members arrive and get settled)	5 minutes	10 minutes
REFLECTION (discuss the opening question for the lesson)	10 minutes	15 minutes
DISCUSSION (discuss the Bible study questions in the Exploration and Reaction sections)	35 minutes	50 minutes
PRAYER/CLOSING (pray together as a group and dismiss)	10 minutes	15 minutes

As the group leader, it is up to you to keep track of the time and keep things moving along according to your schedule. You might want to set a timer for each segment so both you and the group members know when your time is up. (Note that there are some good phone apps for timers that play a gentle chime or other pleasant sound instead of a disruptive noise.) Don't feel pressured to cover every question you have selected if the group has a good discussion going. Again, it's not necessary to go around the circle and make everyone share.

Don't be concerned if the group members are silent or slow to share. People are often quiet when they are pulling together their ideas, and this might be a new experience for them. Just ask a question and let it hang in the air until someone shares. You can then say, "Thank you. What about others? What came to you when you reflected on the passage?"

GROUP DYNAMICS

Leading a group through *Life Lessons from Hebrews* will prove to be highly rewarding both to you and your group members—but that doesn't mean you will not encounter any challenges along the way! Discussions can get off track. Group members may not be sensitive to the needs and ideas of others. Some might worry they will be expected to talk about matters that make them feel awkward. Others may express comments that result in disagreements. To help ease this strain on you and the group, consider the following ground rules:

- When someone raises a question or comment that is off the main topic, suggest you deal with it another time, or, if you feel led to go in that direction, let the group know you will be spending some time discussing it.
- If someone asks a question you don't know how to answer, admit it and move on. At your discretion, feel free to invite group members to comment on questions that call for personal experience.
- If you find one or two people are dominating the discussion time, direct a few questions to others in the group. Outside the main group time, ask the more dominating members to help you draw out the quieter ones. Work to make them a part of the solution instead of the problem.
- When a disagreement occurs, encourage the group members to process the matter in love. Encourage those on opposite sides to restate what they heard the other side say about the matter, and then invite each side to evaluate if that perception is accurate. Lead the group in examining other Scriptures related to the topic and look for common ground.

When any of these issues arise, encourage your group members to follow the words from the Bible: "Love one another" (John 13:34), "If it is possible, as far as it depends on you, live at peace with everyone" (Romans 12:18), and, "Be quick to listen, slow to speak and slow to become angry" (James 1:19).

Thank you again for taking the time to lead your group. May God reward your efforts and dedication and make your time together in this study fruitful for his kingdom.

ALSO AVAILABLE IN THE LIFE LESSONS SERIES

Now available wherever books and ebooks are sold.

ALSO AVAILABLE IN THE LIFE LESSONS SERIES

Now available wherever books and ebooks are sold.